T0198665

I LOVE
Who I Am

IGNITING SELF-WORTH

STORM HIDEAWAY

BALBOA.
PRESS
A DIVISION OF HAY HOUSE

Balboa Press books may be ordered through
booksellers or by contacting:

Balboa Press
A Division of Hay House
1663 Liberty Drive
Bloomington, IN 47403
www.balboapress.com.au
1 (877) 407-4847

Cover Art by Chelsea Lemon

Print information available on the last page.

ISBN: 978-1-5043-0849-6 (sc)
ISBN: 978-1-5043-0850-2 (e)

Balboa Press rev. date: 06/14/2017

CONTENTS

PART 2

Dedicated to my two beautiful
daughters – forever in my heart.

PROLOGUE

The story that unfolds is the story of my life so far.

This is my journey, and while I have encountered pain and challenges, I acknowledge my words as truly my own. I do not want to inflict blame or anger, but rather to share a story that includes heartaches and traumas, with light and hope along the way.

My story is fundamentally about my relationships – with others and with myself. It's about the choices I made and the realisations that finally set me free, yet with a constant, lasting pain in my heart.

Now that I have come this far in my own journey I feel an immense desire and calling from my spirit to share my perspective.

I wanted to share my journey and my insights with other women because I strongly believe my story may help other people – especially those in the community facing similar situations or feelings – to see their own worth and light.

My hope is that these women may relate to my story as a reflection of their own journey.

From there, I want you to see that there is a path and a network of loving, caring and beautiful women in the world ready to help you, as they helped me.

This is my gift to you.

*names have been changed throughout

ACKNOWLEDGEMENTS

To my family for supporting me while I was ill.

In my darkest moments of despair, not sure if I wanted to live or die, I consciously decided to live. I needed to heal the wounds but had no idea where to turn. I searched for answers with desperation.

I can't recall how many times I picked up a self-help book from specialists in depression and trauma, only to place it back down because I didn't believe I could ever get there. I felt I couldn't reach that level of enlightenment they promoted.

Thankfully, I did find some authors who made a difference at the right time and helped me along the way.

To the editor Shae Lalor, it is a credit to her for mending and mastering to deliver the messages and finding balance to set the story free.

Ultimately it is thanks to the people who loved me and were willing to extend a hand. You gave me strength, courage and a belief in myself that keeps me standing strong today.

This book could never have happened without the people that made generous contributions and helped my pozible. com campaign become a reality to self-publish.

I know I would not have been able to endure the pain of reliving the story without the unconditional love and strength of my husband who came up with the idea that I could write a book.

To my daughters, my greatest desire is that you will one day understand what really happened.

PART 1

CHAPTER 1

Negativity attracts

Have you ever felt life is a series of events that seem to attract similar things, whether they be negative or positive? Well, that was my experience. I thought I was on the right path, but what I found was certainly a dark, negative pattern forming. The problem was I never really noticed it was happening.

I was born in Sydney, Australia, in an inner city suburb to a migrant, working class family that spoke broken English with an insistence on speaking Spanish at home.

Looking back, from the moment I was old enough to remember, I compared myself incessantly to everyone else around me. I found it difficult to understand why I couldn't value myself.

I told myself I was not as good as anyone else. Everyone was better than me (and I mean EVERYONE including family, friends and strangers) at something than I was. Call it superficial but this is how I spent many of my years.

> *I still do this sometimes even today. When I start to doubt myself, I question my importance and self-worth and I have to consciously remind myself that I am worthy, that I am valued. Through my journey, I have come to realise that I am not the only one. SO many women today, devalue themselves and do not consider themselves worthy of affection, love, attention or even credit for accomplishments. This needs to change.*

I considered myself to be below average, not smart, not overly attractive.

I was just a kid, but I just did not fit in. To be honest, I felt *worthless* from a very young age.

My inner critic was dark and damaging from the beginning.

CHAPTER 2

My early years

Like most children, school plays a big role during our foundation years. I would go to school, come home and have dinner. I spent most of those years trying to get good grades. There was always the expectation to do better in school.

I remember my first day at school, walking into the school yard with my heart racing. I said goodbye to my Mum and as she walked away, I felt so alone, so abandoned. I tried to stay hidden from attention and not be noticed.

I remember I would slouch in my seat so I wouldn't get picked to take the lunch basket to the canteen. Most kids would put up their hand and yell out, 'Pick me!'.

Why was I so different?

I would dread the days I had ESL study (English as a second language). In the late 1970s, students were separated into a special class for what they called Extra English Support.

I remember it so clearly as if it was yesterday. I would lose concentration easily and find myself looking out the window drifting into my dream place, watching the birds go by when *SLAP*, I would feel the abrupt hand of a teacher across my face. I was so surprised, but more than anything, ashamed.

I was ashamed for being punished, but also for not understanding what we were doing and for not paying attention. The shame was so great I could feel it in my stomach and my throat, but I still tried to swallow the tears and not let people see me cry. Crying made you look weak and was just another thing kids would make fun of.

I felt so alone in school. I sensed all the kids talked about me behind my back and nobody liked me. I felt like nobody understood me.

When I was ten, my parents decided to move overseas to what was then their homeland. This was my cultural home and I looked forward to being surrounded by family and people who were similar to me from a cultural perspective. This was a massive change to enter a Spanish–speaking environment after living in an English–speaking one.

The next three years came and went so quickly.

While I started getting top grades at school, there was still a lingering sense of, *I am not good enough*. Even though I spoke the language, I was still an outsider because I had been raised in Australia. I never felt like I belonged anywhere. I was destined to always being an outsider; to be alone?

I would strive to get better results. I needed to make more friends. I had to please my family more. It just never seemed enough!

This all went on in silence inside me. Some call it ego or fear. It was an inner battle in my mind, a little voice in my head telling me something negative whenever I was about to take a positive action or change.

'Stop, Storm don't do it as it won't work out', or 'Storm, you weren't that good at this last time.'

CHAPTER 3

A distance with my mother

Early memories of my Mum were shadowed by her absence.

I don't remember seeing her often as she used to go out and take care of the family business.

When my brother and I were younger overseas, we lived with my grandmother and had a housekeeper that was more like a family member with us even when we couldn't pay her anymore. There wasn't a lot of money. My Dad was still working in Australia, after we returned overseas for a few extra months to save extra money to bring back overseas for the business. He eventually arrived overseas, which offered us a little more stability for a while.

There were key moments when Mum would stay up at night smoking and worrying where the money was going to come from to buy food and pay the bills. A lit cigarette was all I could see in the dark, smoky room, while she sat and fretted.

The saddest Christmas I had was in 1981. Dad had returned to Australia to prepare for our move back to Australia. We had no money for presents. As a conscientious child, I had worked hard to do well at school to achieve good grades. Yet Santa Claus didn't come with the same generosity this particular year. I couldn't understand. I thought, 'What! Why don't I deserve the doll I had asked for when I have worked so hard for this? Why do I get a puzzle this year when I got a bike last year?'

Inevitably, I questioned my self-worth and dared not to bother my Mum or my grandmother. Dad was too far away to ask.

I did really feel for my Mum. I watched her leave so early in the morning to deal with the business and come back so late, exhausted. There were so many times that I felt that my mum had to work so hard in a declining business and money was so scarce that as a result I did not want to burden her with my feelings or ask for anything for myself.

That's why I bottled my emotions and pretended everything was okay and got on with life. But the pain was real. I recall one time when I wanted a small toy so badly, that I ended up stealing the same toy from a friend at school and never owned up to taking it. Inside of me I knew it was wrong and it made me feel so upset that I would do this to my friend but it was the only way I could have what I wanted without burdening my parents.

I remember one winter living overseas was particularly tough. I was always tense and had caught a cold. Not thinking much of it, I was surprised when my nose began to bleed out of control. Towels and towels became soaked with my blood. My grandmother ran to the nearest neighbour for help as there was no phone at the house.

Mum was out running the business as usual.

In what felt like an eternity, I screamed out to my grandmother from the front door, feeling incredibly afraid. When my grandmother finally returned, she placed a cold compress on my forehead, telling me the ambulance would be there soon.

I had lost so much blood I had no energy to even walk down the balcony and out to the ambulance. The housekeeper carried me out of the house in her arms and I prayed my Mum would come and be with me soon. In that moment, she did arrive.

The journey to the hospital was long and scary, so was the short stay of about two hours. I remember a doctor trying to insert a long pair of tongs in my nose, which I vehemently refused by turning my head and hiding my face in my Mum's embrace.

Our bodies have a way of telling us when something isn't right. My haemorrhaging was the cause of an inflamed vein, which was cauterised years later.

As a young girl entering adolescence, I never felt like I connected deeply with my mum. In my mind I always felt that she had other, higher priorities. There were examples of how she cared about me as well as examples of me not being worthy of her time in my mind. I guess in the end I chose to believe I was not worthy of being loved as it was easier to understand and believe.

CHAPTER 4

Returning to Australia

Overseas, I had finally found some level of stability and felt I was a small part of something – I had some sense of belonging to a community, even though there were times I still felt isolated.

I was looking forward to participating in the school play. I'd made some friends. Things were going well.

Then, due to business issues, my parents made the decision to return to Australia.

I missed out on participating in the school play. It felt as if my family had betrayed me – I was angry at them for taking away my friends and the world I had taken so long to put together.

It was time to start all over again in Australia.

Initially the transition was difficult. At 12 years old, I had to share a house with my cousin's family. Can you imagine four girls squeezed into one very small room, with bunk beds and a single bed? It wasn't easy. We took turns to share the single bed. It was hard.

Sharing a three bedroom house with my cousins was certainly a learning experience. While it lasted less than a year, it taught me life-long lessons on being resourceful and flexible.

After they moved out, my focus moved to adapting culturally to living in a rough area in Western Sydney.

In such a turbulent neighbourhood, you'd see a phone booth vandalised so badly the whole thing needed to be replaced. Our Year 5 classroom was vandalised by a student, who poured purple paint over books, desks, chairs, everywhere!

It was an environment where I found myself having to speak up amongst the kids to survive – although I still hesitated to even put up my hand to ask a question when I didn't understand the work.

I remember a time when I was crying in class. The teacher asked me to come outside. He asked me what was wrong, so I quickly had to make up a story about how I couldn't see the board. In reality, I didn't understand what was being explained, but was too afraid to admit it. I felt stupid and ashamed.

Thankfully, I recall having my first close friend when I was in Year 5. Her name was Debbie.

We were physically really different: she had her long blonde straight pony tails and blue eyes, while I had my dark curly hair and hazel eyes. Yet I finally felt like I identified with, and connected with someone.

15

Making this wonderful connection with Debbie allowed me to embrace Australia, teach me how to eat bangers and mash, get me up to speed with my English and just be a child going over each other's place and play with barbie dolls after school. Debbie, being an only child, enjoyed my company just as much and was happy to share her toys and play in a very girly room where everything was pink. I felt like I had someone I could turn to, I wasn't lonely anymore for that full year.

The following year we moved to a safer suburb and better schools. This year was particularly difficult seeing my youngest brother almost lose his life. We were playing at a park climbing up a rocket with my cousins and aunt. He was 5 years old and while trying to climb down my mother asked me to help him down.

I thought: "he'll be fine, he can do it on his own". I just thought mum was worrying for nothing.

The next thing I know he was on the ground on his side, his head had hit concrete and was in surgery. I remember seeing my mum running down the street with him in her arms trying to find a doctor's surgery. Thankfully he recuperated and made a miraculous recovery. I felt so much guilt over the incident and it again reinforced my self-doubt and lack of self- worth. Why did I have to cause this to my brother? Why did I not listen? Why was I so stupid and selfish?

My brother has always stood firm for me and tells me it was not my fault, but for a long time there was a feeling of guilt if only I had helped him in time I could have prevented the accident from happening. It took me a long time for me to forgive myself for his accident.

CHAPTER 5

Growing up afraid

By the time I got to my senior years in high school my parents had purchased a home. This gave me some permanence – a confidence we weren't going to be moving around so much in the future.

I loved our new house and neighbourhood. Over 90% of the population in our area was either Italian, Greek, Hispanic or Yugoslavian at the time, so I felt right at home. It was satisfying to attend a school where everybody was like me.

Even so, I never found school easy. I struggled with getting my grades. My study of languages was the only subject I was really good at.

My high school years were a mix of fear and facades. With my group of friends, I was the accommodating, quiet, friendly girl always there for them. This was the persona that I lived. I always put everybody else before me. I was the least worthy in the group, so it made sense that I put everyone else first. I was also too scared to take any chances, too afraid to say what I really felt.

My friends saw my fears. A close girlfriend gave me a small plastic card to keep in my wallet for one of my birthdays that said:

> *If you don't do it, you'll never know what would've happened if you would have done it.*

It was a huge reminder of how much I feared life. I couldn't shake this image that was built around fear rather than the real me.

In my late teens and into my early 20s I struggled with acne and it again had a real impact on my self-esteem. I would spend hours in my room looking at magazines wondering why I wasn't the perfection I was seeing in the magazines and began telling myself over and over and over, 'I'm ugly, so ugly I want to die, I want to kill myself.'

I see now it was a desperate cry for help.

My teenage years were a constant struggle with my grades. I would bust myself to achieve straight Cs. Teachers would provide comments like, 'Storm is shy', or 'Storm is a pleasure to teach', or 'A delightful student that always tries her best.'

These comments would frustrate me. I couldn't understand why I couldn't just change overnight. I didn't want to be the shy girl and felt the label placed barriers around me without knowing how to change or ask for help.

When I was 14 years old, my grandmother came to live with us. I felt so embarrassed having to share a bedroom with my grandmother!

Yet her lessons were invaluable.

I spent many mornings playing around, jumping on our old 1970s green bunk bed while she would tell me stories – unsure if I was really listening or not.

She talked about her life back home, her time at the nun's school, and how she was too young to remember losing both her parents. She spoke of how she had become a strong woman.

The thing is, I was listening all that time and cherished what she passed on to me.

She would always say, 'Mijita (short for my little daughter in Spanish), go out into the world, be independent and live your life in the present moment dear.'

She passed away at 99 years of age.

Her lessons are even more poignant to me now.

CHAPTER 6

Pressure to succeed and please

Throughout high school, I concentrated on the only subjects I did well in. I worked hard on my languages and started to get a sense that I would become a teacher.

All the girls I knew seemed to have few expectations about their own futures. I thought they had limiting beliefs, with goals to be stay at home Mums (no disrespect as I wanted this too, but something in me also wanted more).

I always wanted to push myself further.

And I felt pressure to succeed. My parents had sacrificed so much to come to this country, which I was expected to succeed for them.

My parents always told me to work hard, study and achieve what they couldn't in this country. I thought that for them to be truly proud of me, I had to achieve a university degree, which I did, but it didn't make me any happier. If anything it was an achievement primarily to please my parents.

It was only years later I came to realise that my accomplishments didn't always equate with happiness, yet this is what we all want in the end.

I also felt a pressure to please.

I had some supportive school friends and a boyfriend in Year 12, who showed partial interest in me. I say this because it was enough for me to feel some of my emotional needs were being met. I was forever chasing the next happy moment and felt responsible for making the relationship work. I felt I had to give back with gifts to demonstrate I cared.

It was a short-lived relationship as he ended up being gay. He seemed to be with me more for the experience of having a girlfriend rather than because he felt anything for me. I thought I must have done something wrong to attract someone like him – surely there must have been something strange about me and that's why he was drawn to me? This made me feel worthless and reinforced my need to be wanted.

This relationship and many more involved me giving a lot of myself rather than receiving. I was always a pleaser – wanting to give, give, give. I continually sought people's approval, love and time. I did this by allowing others to make decisions for me. I even allowed my parents to do this for me as a young adult.

I believe this need to please stemmed from my upbringing – from my Mum's need to feel in control and due to her own unresolved issues.

I felt I always had to please my parents and was always being judged for everything, and everything I did wasn't ever good enough.

With maturity and the eventual birth of my own children a few years later, I learnt to accept that my parents did the best they could do at the time. I let go of the perception of perfect parenting and accepted a new relationship that encompasses all our mistakes and achievements.

CHAPTER 7

A search for worth

By the end of Year 12, I still had a lingering sense of not being enough. I didn't feel whole, worthy enough, or the person I thought people wanted me to be.

I knew professionally where I wanted to go because my parents had guided me. It was always my dream to be a teacher.

I knew I was good at languages, so my focus was on working hard at that with an expectation that it would fulfil my life. I had centred so much on this vision there was not much thought given to **me** as a person.

And I wanted a family – to find someone that would be loyal to me, that would love me, and to help that someone become a better person.

Initially, I also wanted to travel and see the world. I didn't have a dream of a particular place I wanted to live. I was happy to be near my family.

At age 20, I foresaw my future at 40 as being well-established, financially secure and with a family of my own. The sort of family you look at and think, wow, one day I want to have that: the house, two kids and a big yard.

This was what success meant to me. This is where I expected to find my worth.

Spiritually, spending time at church and having God in my life did offer some help. I wish I had the wisdom I have now, so that I could have focused more on this to fulfil my happiness.

Instead, I searched for fulfilment in others – and particularly in the wrong people.

CHAPTER 8

The path chosen

As a young adult, I hated living with my parents. I had no freedom.

God forbid if I stayed out all night with a guy – I would have never heard the end of it!

I was desperate not to live this way anymore. I wanted out and it seemed the easiest way was to marry someone. This would be considered socially acceptable.

My parents didn't want me to marry the man I chose. Yet their strict upbringing which allowed me few choices for my own freedom even at age 18 deliberately and unknowingly made me go down a path, that in hindsight, I didn't want.

The way they brought me up was all about fear of mistakes that I may make and how to protect me so that I wouldn't ever be hurt. This directly affected my self-esteem. I thought that anything I did I couldn't possibly do as well as they could.

So when I decided to get married, I felt I did not have any other choice.

When I first met Evan it was in my home. My friends Maria and Gus had come around to get some bread and had brought him over and I thought, 'Wow, he's nice, he's friendly.'

Then they invited me to go camping so I joined them. We played cards all night and then watched the sun come up. It wasn't easy to get to know Evan as he was reserved. I took this as a good challenge. I always thought if a relationship was too easy, I would be bored. Now I think the complete opposite!

Life is filled with decisions that determine which path you can take. The mistake we make is to not accept that it was at the end of the day, our choice. I could have taken another path, and it has taken me a long time to admit that. I take responsibility for that now.

CHAPTER 9

Early signs

I dated Evan for about a year around the age of 21. I fell in love and I would spend a lot of time at his sister's place. It was interesting that we never went out to dinner or did fun things. I always thought it was because we had limited funds because he was on a holiday visa and he eventually had to go back to his homeland.

I always thought I was the one that had to make it all work. I'd coordinate our activities and make things happen if I wanted to do anything. I expected when I had my job, it would allow me to *fix* things. Financially, I would be able to afford the things that we weren't able to enjoy or do.

I should have realised things weren't going to change. It should have been obvious to see these habits would offer the same lifestyle later. But that is one of the challenges with life. Hindsight is wonderful and you believe you know it all when you are 21. No one can tell you what you are not willing to see. It would be 15 years later before I understood or would accept this.

In the few relationships I'd had, my track record wasn't good. I tended to choose the most difficult relationships. Any relationship I fell into I had to make work. It wasn't about any guy wanting to sweep me off my feet, I had to work at it. I thought it was always me – that I wasn't *good enough*.

When Evan went back overseas, my challenge was to work at getting him back here. It was very stressful having to do all the paperwork, proving that it was a true relationship with photos, and worrying about money.

To try and help with our financial situation, I took on a job while studying. I used to get up at 3am to clean banks with a friend. My goal was to save for his plane ticket back to where we were living. I did eventually pay for his ticket, so he was able to return. We then had three months to get married and prove that it was a relationship so he could remain here in the country. We married in 1994.

That was how my relationship began.

CHAPTER 10

Ticking the boxes

After we married, I began to develop certain expectations of Evan. I wanted him to work, learn English, assimilate into the community, and support us as a couple.

He started a cleaning job around the time I landed my first permanent teaching job. We rented an apartment and I thought we were going full steam ahead.

Then I wondered, what's next?

We'll buy a house of course, because I expected this next step would equal happiness.

I found it challenging to come home from work, prepare my lessons and then work on the relationship. The first 12 months were tough.

We decided to live at Evan's sister's place to save up for a deposit for a house. The accomplishments we sought were all centred more on materialistic things rather than emotional growth.

In fact, I'm not convinced there was ever an emotional connection. There was never any time or effort put in to making our relationship grow. I never found our relationship deepening.

I started to express more expectations and would hear myself saying, 'You should go and study English and get a trade.'

He always found a reason not to explore more opportunities.

I would look after the mortgage with my salary and he would pay some of the bills. We always had enough to get by. As a result, I believe he never aspired to achieve anything beyond basic cleaning jobs. He was happy to live in mediocrity and was driven by fear.

We did end up buying a block of land and building our house. I watched Evan demonstrate his emotions and feelings through the physical building or working on our home. It was expensive to build the house and it was completely bare inside for some time. All the little extra inclusions were done in small steps.

Evan did much of the work himself by building the pergola, concreting out the back, laying the grass and doing basic landscaping.

I know this was his way of contributing to the relationship.

However the disconnection was already there for me. I craved a deeper level of emotional connection.

Searching for a connection

There was a very clear moment when I was just 25 years old.

I remember getting up out of bed having just had an argument with Evan. Something rang a bell inside me and I thought, 'Do I really want to continue this relationship or should I say goodbye now?'

At the time I was also thinking about growing roots and wanting to have a child. I thought to myself, 'I'll be happy when I settle down and have a child to take care of and then everything will be ok.'

My self-esteem was still so low that I had to physically do things to make myself feel better. I continually convinced myself that all the issues were due to me. Perhaps I was the one not working hard enough in the relationship and I was to blame? There was some doubt, but the doubt was never strong enough because my self-worth was so low, it wouldn't allow me to see things for what they were.

Ultimately, I stayed with the belief that I could make this work.

Growing up I had watched my parents' relationship. It was always tense and regularly a struggle, so I figured marriages weren't easy. I presumed you just have to make it work, although I had never really experienced true love equal to mine. The lack of self-worth stopped me from realising I was worthy of finding that person equal to me, equal to what I was willing to give and commit to.

For Evan, I believe it was easy to be attracted to someone that was willing to give so much. I thought that must be love. And perhaps he didn't know if it was either.

Trying for a baby was a happy time and yet disappointing at the same time. I remember asking my husband if he wanted to come with me to the doctor to hear the news together – perhaps it would be good news or a disappointment – but either way we could share it. He said no. He would just wait at home. It was always no. It was always too hard.

This was supposed to be a really beautiful moment and I had to find out on my own. Those important moments should have been shared with the person that was supposed to put me first.

After receiving the exciting news from my doctor, I came home to share it with Evan. He was happy. Again, I convinced myself that any negative thoughts were my doing, so I shifted the negative thoughts and concentrated on the fact that I had life inside me and this was going to be a new part of our journey together.

I hoped and prayed that being pregnant and bringing a baby into the world would bring us closer together. Deep down what I craved the most was that this would bring out a different side to him. Thankfully, it did.

CHAPTER 12

A new focus

The first 5 months of being a mum was a wonderful bonding time. It was surreal going into hospital to give birth at midnight. It took 3 painful hours from when I got to hospital. I waited in anticipation and wondered if I would have a girl or a boy? Would he or she be healthy? And who would he or she look like?

We named our daughter Cielo. She was a beautiful, happy baby.

I enjoyed making her food from scratch and loved seeing her grow, playing hide and seek, taking her first steps, teething and sleepless nights were all being part of the development of my girl.

She'd enjoy taking out all the pots and pans from the cupboard and rearranging them while I did the chores. She loved going to the park playing on the slippery dip and for me to push her on the swing.

While I witnessed Evan develop into a caring, hands-on Dad, the birth didn't change or deeply impact our relationship – and this is what I wanted most.

Setting up a new home, getting a pet and watching Cielo grow was a wonderful time.

However most of what Evan and I shared together in these early years was a process of acquiring new things: the next car, the pool, our 'stuff'. I thought we needed these things to make our relationship grow.

I would look for the flaws in my environment and convince myself we weren't happy because we were just starting off and life was difficult. If we needed to make sacrifices now, later in life we would have fun and enjoy ourselves more.

Perhaps at that point I was in denial – blaming external things for not feeling complete in my relationship instead of looking inward and seeking therapy.

After only five months of maternity leave, I had to go back to work. Financially I was the primary money earner and we needed to pay the mortgage. This was a pivotal point for me. I resented having to be the one working full-time through the day and then being Mum when I got home in the afternoon.

I really struggled returning to work. Cielo would cry at the window as I left for work each day. I recall my dad saying, 'Let me make it easier for you. I will take her to school and bring her back to make the transition easier.' That was comforting. It allowed Cielo to make the transition and it was easier for me each morning. It also allowed a beautiful relationship to blossom with her grandfather.

Having Cielo settled in the morning mended things for a while, but it was just a Band-Aid. Deep down I still resented leaving Cielo for work and I started searching for other answers. My relationship was in automatic, work was a necessity and I was always tired. I felt terribly alone and I blamed myself for feeling this way.

CHAPTER 13

Continually trying to fix things

This is when we decided to move interstate.

I thought that this change would allow me to have half the mortgage and enable me to stay home. Perhaps we could have another child and that would fix things, fix the relationship.

And yes it did give us the opportunity to purchase a home and me the chance to stay at home. But it did not fix the relationship.

Having another child was beautiful. We named her Chloe and she was my little baby. The day she was born I remember looking at her for hours, she looked as if she was already a month old with her hand out of the blanket peacefully sleeping all night. Touching her tiny hand, kissing her gently, her eyes were so much like mine, it was like seeing a tiny version of me. I remember it was night with plenty of frost outside and watching her till dawn broke.

She was a placid little girl, she enjoyed singing and dressing up in my heels, wearing fairy dresses and dancing around the house making sure she always charmingly had everyone's attention.

But this addition didn't fix us. It didn't change the relationship. The next two years allowed me to bond with my new baby and enjoy being a Mum again, yet this new world was isolating. Evan wasn't open to the idea of meeting new people. This made me feel sad for myself and for the girls.

Around this time I recall an argument we had – and this time he was more than just verbally abusive; he was physically abusive. He grabbed my neck and I panicked. I was out of breath and then he stormed out of the house. Cielo came running and asked, 'What happened? What's the matter?'

All I could do was try and get it together for my daughter's sake. I tried to get my breath back to normal and said to her that it was ok, mum and dad had just had an argument and that was all.

I tried to put it behind me, emotionally putting up a wall to protect myself and convince myself I was overreacting. I made up excuses for him that life was stressful at that moment. Moving interstate and the birth of a second child had placed tension on the family. I had a million excuses in my head to justify his actions and convince myself it wasn't his fault. To tell myself that it was what any normal family had to go through in difficult times and it could always be worse.

These were the first physical signs something was extremely wrong.

Life as a couple was really non-existent. We were cohabitating and raising our daughters, but I was very unhappy. He never made an effort and seemed oblivious to our (or maybe just my) despair.

There were so many events I wish we could have attended together. I would clean the house Friday night and then come early Saturday afternoon, I would walk around in circles and wonder what to do.

Evan certainly never said you can't do this or you can't do that with friends, but I always felt I would be disloyal to him if I did not include him. If he wanted to stay home, then I needed to be home too – for us as a couple.

Frustratingly, we were now finally financially able to afford to do things together. Yet, as much as I wanted to, we never went anywhere or did anything. Our social life was non-existent and at most we would go interstate to visit a couple of friends.

Every now and then we would bundle up the kids and travel all the way to our destination point to then return the same day. Sometimes I just wanted to stay and really spend quality time catching up, relaxing and enjoying the moment. Instead, we faced a six hour drive each time.

I always felt I had to accommodate and make the sacrifice to meet his needs. He needed to be back home to feel secure, but he was not willing to lift a finger and be accommodating for me or anyone else.

One day, I finally convinced him to go on a picnic together. It was something that I always wanted to do with the girls to watch them play and have fun. He was hesitant all the way and would make comments about how it was a dumb idea. We had driven an hour out of town in beautiful countryside looking for a good spot to stop and park. But it got to the point where it was so frustrating to listen to him that I just said, 'OK, you're right. Let's go back.'

I thought, 'Well if I can't go on a picnic in the outside world then I can create a picnic in our own backyard with just me and my girls'.

This way I did not have to inconvenience anybody. All Evan wanted to do was relax on the couch. He was happy when he didn't have to be involved in the activities I organised for the girls.

CHAPTER 14

Getting to crisis point

After Chloe was born we decided to move to a larger home with a bigger backyard. Yet again, I hoped things would improve.

At the same time, it would mean starting work again to pay for the larger mortgage.

Thankfully, working at a wonderful school opened new opportunities for me to feel valued and to practice the virtues I believed in. It was an environment to reach out to many students and develop my skills.

However, after six years of full-time work, being a Mum to two busy young girls, and not having a social outlet to renew my batteries, my life was beginning to feel like too much for me.

I would find myself sitting in front of a computer looking at properties overseas because I thought by going back overseas to his country, it would make him happy and solve my issues. I still wondered if maybe it was just me.

Friends would say to us, 'What you two need is to go away together.' But he never wanted to. I would suggest holidays as a family, but it was always too much effort for him. He was comfortable just staying at home.

Yet deep down inside there was a small part of me – that was getting louder – that would say, 'It's not you Storm, it's him. And no matter what you do, he will never change and he will never make you happy.'

Of course I would still question and blame myself for thinking that way.

A typical day would start with dropping the kids off at school, going to work, coming home, cooking and helping the girls with homework, and then falling, exhausted, to bed. I lived in this rushed, frantic world.

There came a point when I allowed myself to stop. I stopped my fictitious routine.

Finally, one day I had a moment to breathe and it became clear to me.

I knew my world was falling apart because I didn't want this relationship anymore. I knew I wanted out. This led to what I can only call a nervous breakdown. Years of frustration, hurt, anxiousness and relief all rolled into one moment in time.

CHAPTER 15

I deserve to be loved

I spent years trying to improve the relationship; I was continually searching for something that would give us the possibility of being happy – of making him happy.

But was he ever happy? I tried and tried to find ways to have the relationship I always wanted.

The final realisation – or bells that rang in my head – followed a conversation with one of Evan's close relatives. She said to me, 'It's not the country, it's not Australia, it's him.'

Instantly my eyes opened. I finally realised at that moment she was right. It wasn't me, it was him. Nothing made him happy, and nothing was going to make him happy. No matter what I did, where I was in the world, I couldn't make it better. It was who he was.

More than anything, I was upset, hurt and annoyed that it took me 15 years to realise this. Somewhere deep inside, had I really known all along?

On my last birthday I celebrated with him, I asked him if he could take me out for dinner – on a date. Unfortunately he was not interested in going out for dinner. He wasn't interested in being romantic on my birthday. He just wasn't interested full stop!

He threw the credit card on the bench and said, 'Here, go buy yourself something.' Wow, is that all I'm worth? A two-second phrase?

Those last moments were incredibly sad. They made me realise I was worth so much more. He may have loved me once, but he loved me in his own selfish way. I deserved better.

I made the decision on 2 July 2009 to leave my husband. After thinking about it for weeks, I started making plans. I discussed it with my sister-in-law and brother, and knew I had their support to live with them until things settled.

The night before, I packed a bag for the girls. I told Cielo that we were going to be spending the night at my sister-in-law's place and that she would be picking them up from school. I had packed a bag for me and took half of my clothes.

In the morning, Evan would always leave earlier than us, so I placed the things in the car, dropped the girls off at school, and tried to make things as normal as possible.

I was nervous because I knew this was the only way to do it. He would have never *allowed* me to leave.

CHAPTER 16

A frightening departure

I received a phone call from Evan at work that day. He asked me, 'Why are half your clothes missing?' I was too afraid to tell him, I didn't know what his reaction would be, so I said to him with fear, 'You never know when I might need them.'

His words in response were, 'You've got someone else. I'm going to your school.'

He turned up at the school in such a rage. Before he arrived, I told my colleagues I needed their support. It felt like a scene from a movie: they were hiding me behind a door so he could not see me. I didn't know which door to leave the school, but eventually they got me out a back door.

I realised then that he may have already gone to pick up the girls from school, so I rang my sister-in-law and asked her to pick up the girls straight away. However, she was over half an hour away and by the time she arrived, he had already picked them up.

I knew that if I went home, it could become a fearful, dangerous situation. I didn't know what he could do. I took refuge with my brother and asked him to come with me to chat with Evan. Then I rang Evan's brother to be there too because he had been through a separation, and I knew he would be looking out for my husband's wellbeing.

When we got there, the girls didn't want to leave him. For some reason they were protecting their father. I told him it was over and that I didn't love him anymore. I packed some things and even though the girls hesitated, I left with them and stayed at my brother's place.

This was one of the scariest moments of my life. But when I made it to my brother's house and I was away from him for the first time, I felt such overwhelming relief. I felt supported by my family and few close friends. My dad's wise words of encouragement and my mum's acts of service.

In particular my sister, brother and nieces who took us into their home with my girls and showered us with love. I felt supported by my family and few close friends. My dad's wise words of encouragement and my mum's acts of service.

In particular my sister, brother and nieces who took us into their home with my girls and showered us with love. I knew I had made the right decision. For the first time **ever** in my life, I put myself first. I acknowledged who I was and what I deserved in life. I deserved to be treated with kindness and respect and I deserved to be loved just as much as I loved back.

CHAPTER 17

Trying to make it work

We decided we would have a week–about arrangement with the girls. At the beginning, things worked well. The girls started adjusting to the new routine.

Then Evan started breaking the routine and telling the girls he would not be able to look after them that night. Cielo would cry because he had not picked her up and he started to create and plant thoughts in Cielo's head that weren't very positive.

For me at this point, although I had the support of family, I was not coping very well.

I would receive all the house bills. Even though he was still living in the house and I was contributing to the mortgage, Evan would not pay anything towards the mortgage or the former household bills. Everything was in my name and so it was left to me to continue to pay for everything even though I was the one that moved out.

I would worry about the girls because they didn't have all the things they needed. He seemed preoccupied with his own needs to know what to do for the girls. I used to collect the girls from school at the end of the week and find Chloe wearing a skivvy in 35-degree heat.

Evan would repeatedly call me and beg for me to get back with him. It got to the point where I just stopped answering his calls. The situation became worse when I moved from my brother's house and into my own townhouse.

Evan would stalk me. He would come around during the night. I would pretend nobody was home. I would shut all the doors in the hallway and hide in the middle of the house so that he couldn't see me. Sometimes he would knock and ring until I opened the door. I never gave in. No matter how scared I was or how much he threatened me, I was **finally** holding on to my self-worth and reminding myself that I was deserving of love.

No man who truly loved his wife would threaten, stalk and verbally abuse her in the name of love. Never!

From bad to worse

While I never thought it would be possible, the situation went from worse to terrifying.

Evan would wait until I came home from work. He would hide in the bushes and when I would open my electric garage door, he would place his foot underneath it to force his way in. He would barge into my house to search for 'evidence' of another man. He would even open my underwear drawer and rip up all my underwear. He would do some crazy, scary things.

On one occasion, I was out walking around the neighbourhood when suddenly I could hear this distinct noise coming from the accelerator of a car nearby. I know for certain it was my ex-husband's car driving around searching for me. I was quick enough this time to hide amongst the bushes and camouflage so he could not see me.

This horrible scene is so embedded in my head I can still hear it in my head if I hear a similar car engine go by.

My thoughts were, 'I won't be able to go home, so where do I go?'

I knew he would be waiting outside my door until I came home as he had done so many times before. I had a colleague and friend of mine, Diana, who lived nearby. I walked a few more streets, checking behind me that I wasn't being followed, and managed to get to her place. Luckily she was home and he had no idea where she lived.

Diana treated me like a sister. She took me in, offered me her clothes to change into, a warm bed to sleep in and breakfast the next day. I won't ever forget this helping hand.

CHAPTER 19

A healing light

Amidst my confusion, fear and lack of grounding, all I could feel was numbness. When I wasn't numb, I was on an adrenalin rush needing to live every moment on fast-forward to ease the pain I felt in my heart and whole body.

One of the teachers at school had started a meditation class during lunchtimes. I hesitated the first time I went there, not knowing what I was in for. The school's chapel room had been transformed into a half-lit room with candles and chairs. There were about eight students from different age groups and a teacher leading the silent, guided meditation.

I found it difficult to focus at first, but I persisted and participated.

The start of the meditation was simply sitting comfortably on a chair with legs uncrossed, being aware of the body without tension. The meditation teacher rang a dome-type bell, which initiated the meditation by asking us to quietly repeat the mantra ma-ra-na-tha throughout, while also being aware of the silence and simply being.

I didn't feel any different coming out of that session. Perhaps I expected a dramatic change all at once since my anxiety levels were so high, but it was like opening the unknown.

I started a new meditative way of thinking for me and discovering a variety of meditations.

After my long days, I would walk up the mountain near my townhouse and find a quiet spot to sit and overlook the suburbs around. I felt a sense of relief closing my eyes and centring my thoughts on one good thing that had happened that day.

I didn't know it then, but this would be the start of a great healing journey I would practice daily.

CHAPTER 20

Spiralling down

I was in a constant state of fight or flight.

I was living in survival mode.

For the most part I was afraid. All the muscles in my body would be tense. It was an uncomfortable feeling like when you are in a state of shock.

I was like this 24/7 and slept very little.

This went on for a year and a half.

I lost a lot of weight, was sweating profusely, and would have a great urge to burn energy.

I found pleasure in running and going up the mountain every day.

While there, and only there, I managed to stop. I would sit and practice the meditation classes I had learnt from school. Sitting up on that mountain just to be in the moment and meditate would comfort and help me.

Yet life had little meaning for me. At this point I felt so numb, I found myself staying in bed all day, sometimes losing track of time, polluting myself with pain killers that really were a quick fix. They would take away physical pain, but not deal with the root cause of the problem, which was the healing of my inner soul.

The townhouse I had rented was meant to have been my new home with the girls, each with our own bedroom, yet it became more like an empty nest. I would look forward to the changeover day when I was to collect the girls. I would wait with such excitement. I would wait for hours and hours and then they wouldn't arrive. After many phone calls, there was still no arrival from the girls. This went on for several months and their visits became more and more sporadic.

I would feel so empty inside as if my arm or leg had been torn away. Never have I been in so much pain.

This brought about a legal case to fight for formal custody of the girls since there was no possibility of coming to an agreement with their father. I really did not want to go to court as neither of us had the money to do so. All I wanted was to have week–about custody and for us to share the time we spent with our children.

I waited and waited for a court reply that never came. After 12 months of waiting, I approached the court clerk to find out why it took so long. I was advised that my case had been closed. I enquired with the court legal aid who said the matter had already been referred to the judge and I was not present for the hearing.

I found the court had not correctly updated my details when I had moved house 9 months earlier, so I never received any of the paperwork for my hearing.

I was devastated.

I felt so scared and lonely fighting for my girls. I was fighting for a right that was mine from their birth that had now been taken away from me.

This truly felt like the lowest point of my life. Later on I would reapply to the court to have the case heard again, but as far as Evan was now concerned he no longer had to allow me to see the girls. And he made sure I had no visitation at all.

Evan would use this to alienate the girls from me. He would tell the girls that I didn't love them. If I loved them I would come home. He would use the non-court attendance as proof of not loving them. When I would go and try and see the girls after school he would say in front of the girls – 'If you love the girls you will come home with us'. When I refused he would say to the girls – 'See I told you, your mum doesn't love you'.

Evan used every reason, everything that went wrong as proof that I did not love my girls and I was to blame for all their problems.

CHAPTER 21

A life reduced

By this stage I had moved from the townhouse and reduced my working hours to concentrate on getting my girls back with me.

The townhouse was empty all the time and I felt it was a waste of money keeping it. So I moved in with a friend nearby into a small converted garage–come–granny flat that I called the shoebox.

It was big enough to fit my bed, clothes and a kitchenette. At this point, I felt defeated and my thoughts lingered on the beautiful home I once had, with the big pool and many memories of my girls learning to swim and enjoying life's simple moments.

Now, not only were my thoughts and dreams small and dark, but so was the space I was living in.

Helping me move into the shoebox was my family. The physical transition had been easy, but the painful part was at the end of the move, sitting down at a small round hand–me–down dining table. None of us knew what to say. The realisation that my life was now reduced to about 25 square metres was starting to sink in.

I was alone and living in a garage at the age of 39. Could life get any lower? What would come next? What could be worse than living in a shoebox?

I felt betrayed. I had lost everything. I had lost my perfect girls and any materialistic thing I had worked hard for over the past 15 years.

When I look back, I now see it as one of life's great lessons about what is really important in life.

Living in the shoebox was mostly lonely. It comfortably could fit two people and at a pinch, it could fit five. Much of the time I would try not to be there because it did not feel like a sanctuary, it was more like a cave; a cold, small and depressing reminder of where my life was at.

As a result I would work longer hours. The weekends were the hardest. I would spend much of this time at the shopping centres just to be surrounded by people going about their lives. I avoided being on my own. In reality though, even though I was surrounded by people, I was more alone than ever. I would cry for no apparent reason. I could not focus on anything and I would find that hours of the day would simply just disappear without me even realising.

This is when I knew depression had set in.

CHAPTER 22

The black dog

Although not entirely convinced I was depressed, I did notice a strong necessity to spend money on clothes, shoes and to be around people. Not necessarily socialising – just not left on my own.

When I wasn't shopping, I'd be at my favourite park sitting on the grass or taking a nature walk, simply hoping this would give me the clarity I needed or if nothing else, would simply kill the time so I could then go home and sleep.

I needed to use as much physical energy as possible – to the point where I felt exhausted. I needed to be tired enough to fall asleep from pure exhaustion. That's because, when it became dark outside and the day was over, fear would set in.

Occasionally, the days were good.

When I followed my routine of teaching half the week, life was bearable. Although it was still difficult to mask my feelings in order to be brave enough to teach the students.

Then there were days where I let my true, raw feelings come out. On my dark, depressive days I would spend the whole day in bed. It was a very cold winter. I would leave the heater on and put on my electric blanket.

I would numb my psychological pain with prescribed pain killers. I would go through photos I had of the girls and reminisce about what I once had that was taken from me.

There was a sense of urgency to go through the days in seconds. To live in hope of something to change. Part of me wanted to close my eyes and wake up in my past world, just so I could hold my daughters and tell them it would all be OK. Yet within a blink, reality would tell me otherwise and I knew there was no going back to that life or to my girls.

When I was conscious of my sad days I could only manage a thought at a time. Most of my thoughts were just concentrated on the pain, the victim I was, and the pain my girls could be feeling. I wondered if they were lonely, hungry and safe. Did they need me? Of course, in my eyes the answer was always **yes**. This stopped me from sleeping and although I was exhausted from constantly crying, I still could not sleep.

I was in a state of despair – secluding to my private thoughts even when I was in public. I could only focus on one thing at a time. A blank stare into the light was sometimes all I could manage.

I knew I needed to regain ways to find happiness.

I would take long drives down to the beach or out to the country where I could just rest in thoughts of nothing – a type of meditation. I didn't know then the extent to which this was helping me.

And living in the shoebox also gave me an opportunity to get closer to my dear friend Kim, who I have grown to love immensely. Kim rented me her garage and became a steady support in my life. Sharing a similar path to mine gave us the strength to pull through the difficult moments together.

I was not alone.

CHAPTER 23

Pawns in a sad game

Although legally I still had the opportunity to see my girls, Evan used the lack of my court appearance previously to justify not giving me any visitation and I as much as I tried he would never allow the girls to stay with me.

The only time I would see the girls was when he used them as part of his psychological games. I recall not long after my move into the shoebox, that the girls came around for the first time. It was a random time they were meant to be with their Dad.

It was late at night. They yelled at me from the gate to come out, begging me to come back and live as a family in my former house. I didn't have the strength to come out and confront their father and hear the same thing over and over. More than anything I wanted to have the girls in my life, but surely there was a better way?

It didn't help that the metal garage I called the shoebox was cold and had poor lighting. In my mind I felt alone and could see no way out.

This would occur over and over again. At times I would come out to the girls at the gate. They would say, 'Come back Mamá, let's be a family again.'

My response was always realistic and rational, yet emotionally I felt broken. I felt as if I was hurting them and disappointing them by saying, 'No sweetie, I won't be going back there, but you always have a home with me anywhere I live.'

Chloe and Cielo could never accept my answers. They were angry their family had been torn apart and had no desire to live anywhere else but their old family home.

I felt the girls were part of a chess game where Evan was playing the game and they were pawns on the board. There was no way of winning.

If only he could see they were the ones that needed to win; they needed to be looked after with our differences put aside.

I found myself constantly having to explain myself and the explanations never made any sense to them because they only wanted to hear one answer: Mum is getting back together with Dad.

Sadly, this was never going to happen.

CHAPTER 24

Getting my life back

Eventually, I started looking for love again.

I took a big step in putting myself out there on an online dating service. I had met a number of potential partners, but none of them seemed to truly capture my heart.

I realised during this time I was seeking answers in the wrong places. It gave me comfort to know I was meeting new people and giving my self-esteem a boost, but I wasn't feeling fulfilled. The pleasure of a man's company, the physical touch and intimacy was only satisfying for a short while.

I met a nice man named Milton online who I became close with during the summer of 2009–10. I realised then that not all men were self-focused and preoccupied with their own actions. I found out that men could be caring, giving and generous with their time, and as a result, my life started to have new meaning.

For the first time in many years, someone cared enough about me to show me what I hadn't experienced before. It was a surreal experience at first. I still found it difficult to believe that I was worthy of being loved and being happy.

I looked forward to spending time with him at the start of a weekend on a Friday evening after work. The rack of wine was full of the finest wines to open, yet none of them appealed to me, so he would have a bottle in the fridge selected especially for me.

I was forever entertained by being taken out to the finest restaurants, musicals and beach getaways. I wondered when the 'evil' Milton would hurt me.

Well he never did.

His home was meticulously clean and tidy with just enough belongings to feel comfortable. There was always music in the background when I arrived, gifts, flowers and a welcoming hug from a somewhat lonely heart.

If there was ever a man that had given of himself completely, it was Milton. Going away at the end of that summer with him was something I'll never forget. His warmth and simple words allowed me to open up and enjoy the romance of walking along the beach, sitting by the pool and just simply capturing the sunsets together. He allowed me to trust men again.

As much as I wanted to believe in the relationship – in the practical world, he was everything I needed to give me moral support, financial freedom and guidance – he lacked the one thing I still craved: love.

I wasn't prepared to waste time (again) convincing myself that it would work. I knew that as much as I loved spending time with him and being with him that I did not love him. In being true to my heart, as well as his, I ended the relationship in early 2010.

CHAPTER 25

A relationship set-back

After my separation with Milton, I began a relationship with a committed man whose partner was overseas.

Although I was getting the physical affection from Adam I longed to have, I was never the primary focus of this man's attention. I was always the other woman, which I had sworn I would never be.

We always had meetings in clandestine places and were wary of being seen when we were in public. I had attracted a man that was half-heartedly involved with me and someone else at the same time.

I knew after the relationship with Milton, I was letting myself down, yet it was almost like an addictive relapse.

I needed the constant contact to have someone demonstrate he cared for me.

I recall a time we went for an autumn walk by the lake, playing with the leaves – kicking and throwing them up in the air, feeling like a child again. For a moment I could leave my concerns, my aching heart, and release the inner child in me.

I was so happy to be dining out with him, to laugh, share stories, and ride on his Vespa holding him tight as if I was 16 again.

Yet I knew this would be short-lived, not knowing how long it would last and when someone would find out about us. Secretly I wanted people to know in the hope he would choose me over her and be loved entirely by this man. I thought that being loved by this man would save me from all the pain I was feeling.

There was a time I lay clothed in his bed because I did not want to leave. I was so afraid of having to return to an empty nest and be on my own again. I did not know when I would be followed or harassed again by my ex, or by the girls. I felt so alone and afraid if I was not with anyone.

At one point, he asked me to please hurry up and leave as he needed to start his work day early the next day. I quickly got up and left his house, holding back the tears. I felt so much shame, pain and disgust in myself for allowing this to happen, and again asking myself if I would ever be good enough for anyone.

CHAPTER 26

The doors re-open

At this point I was so exhausted from this emotional rollercoaster of going from one relationship to another that I finally spent time just focussing on me. I had to learn to feel comfortable just spending time with myself.

What I discovered is that being on my own wasn't as bad as I had thought.

I took advice from a girlfriend to always take a book with me in case things got too uncomfortable when alone. This worked. I didn't feel the need to jump out of my seat and run off as I normally would, and started to enjoy my own company without the feeling of loneliness. I didn't need to have someone with me because I was never enough.

I was starting to live in the moment, to feel every part of my body without the fight or flight response.

I was beginning to enjoy being around people. In my old life I had to go out shopping and spend money just to feel alive and worthy of something. Now as I started to feel good about myself again, I was able to go out shopping simply for the enjoyment, not for the need to feel something.

Spending time with myself, out for long drives, enjoying the natural scenery and going on nature discoveries in absolute silence with just the wild birds as my company was immediately healing. This made me feel alive again, born again with a small light inside me that began beating.

Feeling my body on the earth and allowing myself to be physically grounded, breathing without pain, smelling the eucalyptus leaves, the mist touching my face, hearing the wind, my feet crushing amongst the leaves. It all gave me a sense of healing and a realisation of a whole world in front of me.

I felt as if nature had embraced me like a blanket, caressing me, loving me to the point I felt we were one. Without words I could feel a new opportunity open its doors to live a quality life.

My heart was filled with warmth. I felt it race with a glimpse of excitement and hope as tears fell down my face. I could feel the energy being reflected back and forth between me and Mother Nature. It was then I knew I would fall many times, make many mistakes, have heartbreaks and achievements, yet there would be no going back to the darkest of moments where I had considered suicide.

I got back in the car to drive home. I was energised and for the first time in so many months, I had found enough love within **me** to keep on going with my journey.

CHAPTER 27

Date with destiny

Online dating was becoming more of a chore. I found it tiring and boring and was about to give it up. After some thought, I decided to give it one last round.

During this time I came across the profile of a man who appeared to be hiding behind a pair of sunglasses in his photo. I was intrigued so sent him a friend request. Steve politely said yes and we began to communicate via email.

He was very honest and mentioned he was overseas with the Navy so there appeared no possibility of starting a relationship – I just thought this man needed a friend. He seemed lonely and I was willing to focus on someone else's need for long distance friendship.

The dating site communication shortly became conversation via email which I looked forward to daily. Steve then began calling me and soon I became very familiar with what was happening in his everyday life, his interests, his past and what he was looking for in a partner.

There were plenty of questions unanswered at this stage and I knew I would not get the answers until I found myself spending time physically with this man. What I did know is that I could take my time to get to know him. I was being the friend he could confide in from a distance. And there was renewed hope that I could meet the person I was looking for, the person that I could share my new life with. I saw again that love did exist.

After a number of weeks of long conversations, Steve surprised me by telling me he would be returning to Australia sooner than anticipated and he wanted to set up a date to finally meet. I can't begin to say how nervous I was! It was as if I was 16 again going on a date for the first time.

We had set up dinner early in the week and I remember finding it difficult to book a restaurant that would be open. Finally I found a nice Italian place on 19 October 2010. A day I will never forget.

I tried on about 10 different outfits, asking for my girlfriend Kim's advice. Is it too dark, too short, too long? And finally I settled for a winter dress and heels. She had asked whether I wanted to come through to her house to wait to be picked up, so we spent some anxious minutes sitting on her porch giggling away like school girls.

Steve arrived punctually, walking up to the veranda and nervously saying, 'Hello, you are so much prettier than in the photos.' I smiled and felt a touch red in the face. I checked him out from head to toe. Steve walked up to the car and opened the door for me.

I remember sitting at the restaurant doing most of the talking while he sat and listened patiently until he asked if he could kiss me. I said yes.

I don't know how many hours we were at the restaurant; we were the last to leave and it felt as if it had been only 15 minutes. Conversation just flowed and we felt so comfortable with each other. The initial seconds of anticipation when we had first met we were both nervous, yet the rest of the evening went so smoothly, it felt like home.

You know when a relationship is right when it all takes place so easily.

CHAPTER 28

Worthy of love

The relationship grew from there and we would spend many weekends together. We were also just as happy to check through our everyday chores together. Steve was recently separated and he had a 14 year old son, Harry.

I used to do a lot of the talking – in fact I probably still do – especially when I was excited to tell him about my day, event or simply laugh about something silly together. He was patient and would listen intently.

By doing this it allowed me the opportunity to open up more and truly trust in him, especially since my belief in men was limited. When I shared negative comments about men, Steve would say, 'Not all men are like that.'

I found out more about him and the deeper feelings and connection: exactly what I searched for in a man. In some ways it was as if I was young again – full of life, hope and desire.

At the end of 2010 I had planned an overseas trip to revisit my cultural roots again where my older brother lives. I was able to spend time with him and his family, do some sightseeing, relax and be in contact with a part of me I wanted to find and explore. This time away allowed me to question if there was ever a possibility of making this place my home like it was when I was a girl.

I found the answers I needed to move on quickly and know that as much as I had enjoyed my stay, home was Australia, where my family was, in particular my girls.

Upon returning to Australia, I was met at the airport by this wonderful new man.

Steve told me he was excited to see me arrive home. I began to ask myself why was this man willing to be by my side against any adversity life was going to throw at me? Do I dare dream and hope that someone was willing to love me? Me! Was I worth it?

We spent three days away before returning home. He had planned a surprise photoshoot with professional hair, makeup and props for the two of us. The truth is at this point in our relationship, I was excited to see him and spend time together but I wasn't yet in love with him.

I certainly wasn't used to being pampered so much. I actually felt uncomfortable at times being the centre of his attention and being thought about so much. He wouldn't even let me lift a finger!

My sister-in-law from overseas would say to me, 'Let yourself be loved Storm, you deserve to be treated right.'

I just had to learn how to feel worthy of love.

CHAPTER 29

Missing my girls

With the holiday over and the trip back home complete, the reality of the situation with my girls soon sunk back in.

My visits to see the girls and communicate with them again was so hard. Here I was visiting the girls in their house where I would only be allowed to stand at the front door for them to say, 'We don't want to be with you, leave!'

I handed over the things I had bought them from overseas, swallowed my tears and left. I thought maybe it was because I was away for the holiday, but this behaviour would go on for years.

My visits were a double-edged sword. On one hand I was experiencing an immense rejection from the anger in their words and hatred directed at me. Yet beneath this were two fearful young souls reaching out for help. They didn't know how to ring the alarm bells for attention to be heard. And I needed to see them, no matter the consequences.

Eventually the school year started and brought with it a much needed distraction. I enjoyed going back to work as it allowed the day to pass quicker, enabling me to spend less time worrying or thinking about the girls. As much as I tried to communicate with their Dad or to even just have the girls come outside and spend a few minutes with me, all I received during that summer was a door slammed in my face.

It was particularly difficult on occasions including Mother's Day, their birthdays, my birthday and Christmas. These were the times I wanted to erase from the calendar, to pretend the dates didn't exist. I wanted to medicate myself to sleep so the day would pass unannounced.

The worst denial was pretending my children were dead. After all they weren't in my life so the pain was more bearable if I could mourn them rather than accept the rejection. I couldn't deal with the agony I felt inside. I would imagine a tombstone with their names engraved where I would visit them and lay flowers for them to rest and ask for peace. Surely this was a better way of living?

On more rational days, I would work on myself and this seemed to soothe the pain. I would worry about Cielo's overload of responsibility and Chloe's feelings of neglect. I still felt like I had a straitjacket on and wanted to yell to the world, 'Release me, give me back my freedom and my children.'

In order to keep my sanity and not return to a state of depression I would spend much of my time with Steve. Half of the time was at his home, which became more and more familiar to me. He had asked me to move in with him once before, and although part of me wanted to, the fear of having to trust a man to that degree terrified me so much that I said no.

I spent much of this time back and forth from the shoebox to his place. A few months later Steve pointed out to me that I was practically living with him anyway and asked again for me to move in. This time it felt right and I accepted.

The two things I loved the most were the warmth of a family meal gathering at the dining table in the evening and a hot shower with continuous hot water for longer than five minutes. Boy, I did not miss that lukewarm shower in winter in the shoebox!

CHAPTER 30

Fighting to be in their lives

On the days I wasn't teaching, I would visit the girls' school. Cielo, who was now 12, didn't want me to visit her at all. On the other hand, Chloe who was just 8, slowly warmed up to my visits and she would eagerly await them. She enjoyed sitting on the oval at lunchtime on my lap.

These visits became more and more frequent and we both looked forward to spending quality time together. In the final week of the first term, I received a call from Chloe that she wanted to come and spend the holidays with me. I was overjoyed. For the first time in over 12 months I would be able to spend some time with my daughter. We decided I would pick her up early from school on the last day so she could come and stay with me without her father knowing.

Friday 8 April 2011 is a day I will never forget. I was so excited I couldn't think straight from the anticipation. The day she arrived there were mixed emotions – she felt happiness and excitement, but was fearful about what would happen when her father found out.

That Friday afternoon I received a call from her Dad wanting to know where Chloe was. I told him she was staying with me for the holidays because she wanted to spend some time with me. He was furious. He demanded to speak with Chloe. I put the phone on speaker so she could hear him. He yelled at her and called her a 'traitor' and said she had no right to be there. She was in a lot of trouble for visiting me. Chloe began crying so I stopped the phone call. I told Evan that she had every right to spend time with me.

During the next couple of days we went by her father's house to collect some clothes. She was yelled at and again called a traitor by her father. He would not allow her in the house to collect her things. He grabbed a bag of clothes from inside the house and threw it at her feet. Despite this incident, Chloe enjoyed the time she had with me over the holidays.

During the Easter weekend we went camping together at a medieval festival with friends. Chloe came along and she really enjoyed going on her first camp. I quickly sewed together a long pink dress which lacked detail, yet to her, she felt like a princess. She even got to go horse riding for the first time. I remember she could not stop hugging and kissing me, almost like trying to make up for lost time.

In our time together, I watched her reading and times tables improve.

It was a fabulous three weeks.

I still feel Chloe's warmth and her caresses from that time to this very day.

CHAPTER 31

A fragile arrangement

Just after the Easter holidays, whilst Chloe was staying with me, Evan decided he wanted to return to his homeland for three weeks. I informed him that Chloe could stay with me while he was away. I also wanted Cielo to stay with me, but he would not allow it. Cielo stayed with her aunt and cousins instead.

My initial reaction was of course disappointment as I would not be able to spend time with Cielo. At the same time I was excited at the opportunity to have Chloe stay for another four weeks as finally I would be able to nurture my little girl and reconnect with her. It was an amazing feeling to know she would be spending time with me.

When Chloe first came to stay with me, she was so excited. The room we had set up for her was finally filled, not just with the things I had purchased for her, but also a loving energy between mother and daughter I cannot explain in words.

Mother's Day was so special that year. I had left aside my pain of not having Cielo in my life and celebrated with joy my little girl's love for me. Chloe had purchased a few items from school from money she had saved. She woke me up with a beautiful card and gift I still have put away in my memory drawers. I can still recall her happy smile and red cheeks. (It is the only Mother's Day I have had with my girls since 2009)

Spending this time together gave me the opportunity to get to know my daughter at a different stage in her life; as an eight-year-old instead of the six-year-old I had once known.

Sadly, there was a lingering feeling that at any given point, this could be taken away from me.

Chloe's time with me had given her some stability that she needed, although she was missing her sister deeply. She would talk about her a lot when she would come home from school.

There were moments she felt content and happy to spend time with me and then there were times her mind would drift off daydreaming with sad eyes because she missed the other part of her family. It was all or nothing and her Dad had made it clear that she wasn't allowed to spend the time with both of her parents.

On 10 June, Cielo had her birthday and Chloe wanted to go back on the weekend to see her sister and wish her happy birthday.

I was planning to pick her up from school the next day and I got held back at work by 10 minutes. When I arrived, I proceeded to get out of the car and walk towards her classroom. From a distance, I saw Chloe walking towards me, and as I got closer she wouldn't speak to me.

I asked her what was the matter and why she didn't want to talk to me and if she was ready to come home with me. Chloe quickly walked up to the car where her father was and got in his car and looked at me from the window with a great amount of fear. At that moment I couldn't understand what was happening. I waited to see if there was any response or comment but there was nothing. I turned to face her father to confront the situation. He looked at me with disgust with the window wound up; I could not speak with him. I didn't say a word, I waited until the car drove off and then I left for home. I began to cry. I felt shattered.

I could not comprehend how this was happening again! How quickly Chloe had been convinced to get in the car and leave.

Chloe missed her sister so much and all she wanted to do was to go and visit her for her birthday. On the Sunday before taking her to see Cielo, one of the last things she said to me was, 'I love you Mummy, I promise I'll be back.'

It never happened. It would be three long years before she was allowed to spend another night with me.

CHAPTER 32

Visits to school

The weeks following Cielo's birthday, I pulled myself together and built up the courage to visit Chloe in the only place that was safe enough: school.

Initially she didn't want me around, so I would sit in the classroom and just watch, occasionally engaging with the other children in the class. This would get her attention and she would watch from a distance. Then slowly we started to talk again and spend time together. This was always precious, limited time.

Chloe would always tell me I was not allowed to be at the school, that her Dad said that I was not allowed to see her. She was frightened that she would get into trouble again. Chloe said that her Dad told her I was no longer her mother and that the courts had taken away my privilege to see her.

She also told me that she had a new Mum now. She said Daddy and Rowena would be her parents and that she was to call her Dad's new partner Mum.

I was devastated at this news and cried for days.

Steve was so supportive and encouraged me to keep going back. To keep being there for her and continue showing her no matter what, I was going to be there because I loved my daughters so much.

Some days were really hard, because Chloe would be so rude and angry that I was there. Other days, she would be happy and excited to spend time with me. Over the year, she gradually began to feel safe that her Dad would not find out. I was always careful to make sure that I was not near the school before the end of the day, just in case her Dad showed up early to collect them. I always told Chloe that she was welcome to come back at any time and be with me.

In September for her 9th birthday, I made her a cake to take into school. We sang Happy Birthday and celebrated in the classroom with a mini-party. I got to take in her birthday present, which was a life-like 'reborn doll' I had painstakingly and lovingly handmade, a card and the present wrapped in a pink bow. Her excitement and happy smile was beautiful. Those days I will never forget.

I would also go in to help her read and sit by her side just to share her day.

She loved this.

Chloe's Year 3 teacher was amazing. I will be forever thankful to him for being so supportive and giving me this opportunity to share these precious moments with my daughter.

CHAPTER 33

Trying to be Mum

Things progressed better from there and I would visit Chloe twice, sometimes three times, a week whenever I could spend the time without major disruptions to the class and have an opportunity for interaction with her.

Chloe began to trust me again knowing she was able to be herself with me without feeling she was doing something wrong by being with me. I would spend lunchtime with her. Sometimes she would play with her friends, but most of that time was spent with me so we could be Mum and daughter. She was willing to sacrifice this free time with her friends just to be with me.

Sometimes she wanted me to watch her at the monkey bars, share with me her accomplishment of finishing a certain book, or show me a picture she had drawn.

This was the highlight of my day. I could be a Mum again to my beautiful girl.

When I would visit Chloe, we would leave the classroom some days and go back home just so we could have some time alone. Chloe would just adore this. Her face would light up with joy and excitement. It was the simple things like making her lunch and sharing stories of what had been happening and the things she wanted to do together.

Simply being able to walk into her bedroom and play – she loved it.

At this point in time, I put all my energy and focus into working out a way to be able to spend more time with both of them. I wondered how to do it. I would frequently ask myself the question, 'How do I get them to see I love them?'

I wanted them to know it was OK to love their Mum and their Dad at the same time, even if we were no longer together.

Some days I would leave home and be on a high. I'd be feeling happy but then get to the school and Chloe was absent. I would try to visit both of them at their father's place and they would never let me in or want to come out. I had no access. Cielo would shout out, 'Leave now!'

I would come back home absolutely shattered, in pieces, defeated and facing uncertainty about where to go from there. I had always considered myself a fighter, but I just didn't know how to fight for them. Emotionally it was so draining I had no energy left in me to come up with a solution – to do something to improve the situation.

It was a rollercoaster of despair. It gives me a knot in my throat just thinking about it now. There were moments that were so very depressing.

In 2011, Cielo was starting Year 7 and there had been an expectation that Cielo would go to the same school where I taught at. I had planned to pick her up, take her to school with me and then bring her back home, but her Dad didn't allow it.

Cielo seemed in favour of this idea as the majority of her friends went to the school where I was teaching and it was the private feeder school. At the beginning of the year I bought her the school uniforms and school supplies. To me there was no other discussion and all was going to plan.

But the day she was meant to start school, she didn't show up. Her Dad had enrolled her into a public school. I had paid a full year of school fees, purchased all the uniforms, text books and everything needed for the year, so there was no financial burden on them, but he did not let her come.

I believe this was a direct attack on me from her father. He did everything he could to make sure I did not have any connection or time with my daughters at this age.

It would be years before I could have contact with them every day and it was only to take them to school because he could no longer do it.

Some days I would gather my strength to go and visit Cielo. In reality, it was only a glance from outside the school classroom or watching her from a distance at lunch time.

It was heartbreaking.

CHAPTER 34

End of a career

There was place that served as a constant reminder of my girls: my own classroom.

I was teaching students who had spent time with Cielo at my home – this was extremely difficult. Occasionally, some of them would ask me where Cielo was. To answer this question without breaking down was desperately hard. I missed her so much. Not only did I miss her as a Mum, but I could also see the benefits she would have encountered coming to this school and being around her friends in a caring and nurturing private school. To suddenly have this choice taken away, just because of our circumstances, wasn't fair on her.

I was her Mum but never saw her. It was painful every single day.

I realised then that teaching for me was over. It was a difficult decision but, I would see these girls and would see my daughter in them. Yet she wasn't there when she was meant to be there.

Not having both of the girls in my life had taken its toll. I finished teaching towards the end of 2011 and then found my depression set in again and to stay for the long term.

Sometimes I wondered how I continued to teach all those years. How did I miraculously stand in front of a classroom, day in and day out, and teach under those circumstances?

Before a lesson of a morning, there were times I would say to my colleagues, 'I don't want to live, I don't want to be here, I don't want to be in this body any more, I want to die.'

They would offer support and tell me that I'd be OK.

This is how I would get through the day. I would try and take what I could with the support I'd been given.

Even with support and love in my life, I had reached rock bottom.

Focus on the simple things

It was doing little things daily that made a difference at this time.

I did not take antidepressants, yet in hindsight it may have been a good idea. Unfortunately I felt this would diminish my options for getting custody of my girls.

Instead I refocused on meditation.

I used my inner circle of friends, colleagues, my psychologist and my partner to gain back the strength to cling on to life.

The love for myself (although I didn't know it at the time) and for my children was keeping me alive.

Even though I had faced the reality of wanting to suicide, I had to continue demonstrating my love for – and to fight for – my girls. I had to battle for a better life for me.

I was in such a bad way, but I needed to learn to love me for who I was in order to be the best Mum I could.

Funnily enough, when I think back over the few moments I had with the girls, one of the things that kept me going in 2011 was an upcoming photoshoot that Steve had bought for me and Chloe. I had wanted to do a photoshoot since autumn when Chloe was staying with me. But it didn't happen then.

Now with Chloe starting to trust me again, I thought we could make it work. Timing was always tricky but we finally settled on a day in late spring for it to go ahead. Flowers had blossomed, all the trees had their leaves and everything was green. It was a beautiful sunny day.

I had asked Chloe to pack a dress and it had a little tear in it. She said, 'That's all I have.' It was a beautiful white macramé dress my mother had bought for her a while back, but it still fit her nicely. I repaired it for her.

I picked Chloe up from school and she got changed at the plant nursery next to where the shoot was going to take place in a lovely park.

It was such an easy and natural thing to do. Some of the photos were posed and others just captured our spontaneity from a distance.

It made me feel like I was on top of the world and anything was possible. My thoughts at that moment were, 'Everyday should be like this.' I wasn't able to understand why this couldn't be, when it was our right to be mother and daughter.

My favourite picture, one that I keep close to me and look at every day, is where I am piggybacking Chloe. She loved me doing that and it's one of our favourite pictures.

CHAPTER 36

Last effort

At the end of the shoot, we went back to my house. Chloe was so excited from the event she wanted to continue the fun as long as she could. There wasn't a lot of time left before the end of the school day and she just didn't want to leave the house to go back to school. I tried to stretch the time limit as much as I could and then said we needed to leave as we would be late.

We arrived just three minutes after the bell. As I drove into the carpark to drop her off, Cielo was walking in front of the parking lot and saw Chloe and I together in the car.

Chloe knew she would be questioned by Cielo and her Dad, so she started to scream and cry. The first thing Cielo had done was ring her Dad.

By the time we returned to the classroom, Evan was there and he was questioning the teacher about why I had taken Chloe out of school without his permission. He said I had no rights to see my daughter. The Principal was called and Evan also questioned him.

At the end of that school year, Evan made the decision to take Chloe out of the school and enrol her in the school across the road. He didn't tell me this. He wanted full control. I wasn't even listed as the other parent when he enrolled her into the new school. I only discovered this when I visited the school office, finding out there was no record of me as the parent.

To gain access, I had to bring in Chloe's birth certificate to prove I was her mother and her legal parent. It was a strange, confusing feeling of being denied a right to see my daughter, and

I felt like I was being punished for no reason.

After this, Chloe became distant and as time progressed, awfully distrusting. I tried to build a relationship with the new classroom teacher, who was very helpful. I would again sit in to help the students and watch Chloe from a distance. She would pull faces and when no one was paying attention whisper, 'I hate you, go away.'

The situation became worse to the point that I decided it was best to not visit as often. I was in so much pain. Going into the classroom was so difficult. I would swallow my tears when Chloe would say nasty things to me.

Worst of all I knew how much she was hurting too. Her lips would say one thing but her eyes could never lie to me. Her sadness was so real. I felt her pain and would ask myself, 'How else can I help you? How can I take that pain away from you and me?' There were no answers at that moment.

With Steve's help and financial assistance we came up with a plan to return to court and fight for the girls a second time. Part of me was against this idea but after some professional advice, I felt I needed to demonstrate to my girls that I would never give up and this seemed to be the only way at that time.

After some long consultations with my lawyer to rebuild the pieces and retell the painful story again, we took the matter to court. The preparation time took days, however the time in court was brief. Although the judge supported my story and stipulated that the love for my children was evident, the majority of the time was to be spent with their father given the children did not want to be with the mother.

Even though I could demonstrate that Evan was deliberately alienating me from my girls, proving parent alienation in court is extremely difficult.

I left the court that day defeated. A knife had been stabbed through my heart and again I had no direction. I had lost all belief in the court system and any chance of ever getting my girls back.

By this point, I had nothing left. I realised then I had to give any remaining energy to myself, to restore the love in me and to learn to love myself again.

All I could now hope for was to be a distant example to my daughters in the hope that one day they would grow up and be mature enough to realise the truth. What I wanted more than anything else at this moment was to become the best version of myself. To prepare for the day my girls would come back and say, 'I love you Mum'.

CHAPTER 37

Trying to grow my nest

Ever since I was a little girl, I would love to play with dolls, dress them, look after them and play with them as if they were my own children.

I felt extremely blessed and grateful when my two daughters were born and really embraced the role of motherhood.

When the girls were not with me and we had established a solid relationship with Steve, we began exploring the possibility of having another child. It wasn't originally in my plans, but once I knew I had been given a new opportunity to form a family again, we started planning a child together.

At first Steve thought of it as crazy. He had his future planned and was almost at a point in his life with his son where he would be independent so he could take on some of the plans he had left aside.

However, the more he saw my unhappiness and thought about it, this vulnerable, giving man was willing to put himself out there for me, just to ensure my contentment.

My relationship with Harry, Steve's son was distant at first. I had opened up to him wanting him to accept me as just his father's partner but it was all too much for Harry. He had his own issues to face trying so desperately hard not to need his mum since she had decided to re-establish herself interstate and only seeing each other during the holiday school breaks. He was also becoming independent and detaching himself from that motherly love he once needed as a boy.

Steve had already been through a vasectomy in his first marriage and had closed that door off for good. I started researching statistics and all the possibilities to be fertile again at age 40. I began to unravel a whole new cyber world of frustrated, upset women who desperately wanted a child and their only escape was an anonymous chat line. I felt so guilty for wanting another child when here were all these women wanting just **one** baby.

My amazing man went through the reverse vasectomy operation to see if we could fall pregnant. Then we needed to wait months before he healed to start trying. Sadly we found out that the sperm was now covered in antibodies, a common occurrence after a vasectomy reversal. So we took the next step, IVF, with a fertility clinic.

I began this search for anything that would help me achieve this dream. There was so much time spent in preparation and anticipation. Was it going to work out? What else could I do to improve my chances? I even

I LOVE WHO I AM

considered the possibility of going overseas. The calendar was covered in reminders and dates when I needed to take herbal tonics and visit a fertility acupuncturist.

I had no idea what I was in for and felt as though I'd be judged for my age, for wanting a child so badly. I thought I would be criticised for spending my time and focus on the IVF journey instead of taking the matter of my girls to court again. But I also thought about the possibility I could give this new life and so I started researching the different clinics, costs and what this meant.

I had it all figured out, I just needed the money I didn't have!

My dear friend Kim could see the anxiety and sadness I felt and had been with me all the way. Without even asking, she lent me the rest of the money I needed to get started.

Steve and I had so much going against us. Our ages and the vasectomy reversal didn't dampen our hope. I would spend my time reading the endless blogs and stories on anonymous online sites where these brave women would talk about their longing for children. They discussed their sadness for their miscarriages and disappointments after getting their hopes up each month of trying and then receiving the news there was no positive result.

After endless weeks of having my body disrupted and challenged with a mountain of drugs, probing and waiting, we finally had three possibilities. We waited patiently for these oocytes to mature, yet on the day of the in vitro fertilisation procedure, we had only one viable oocyte.

This was it, it had to be. We prayed and hung on to dear hope that it would grow to be an embryo and we could finally be pregnant. I had all the signs of being pregnant and then went in for that final blood test – so wanting it to be positive. Unfortunately we received the sad news it was not to be. It was yet another disappointment and all that hard work with no results.

We had only told two people, so it felt so strange and lonely. We were mourning a child that wasn't to be in complete silence.

I tried to focus on keeping my mind occupied until finally I reached a point I had to face reality. In the coming months we made the decision we wouldn't try again.

I felt sadness for what wasn't to come – for the little girl Steve would never call his daughter, or the son I would never have.

Yet I knew deep down I couldn't withstand both financially and emotionally such a challenging journey without any secure outcome.

I needed to find another path, the one God and the universe had set out for me.

PART 2

These are my learnings.

These are the actions that helped me heal from my depression and improve my self-worth.

I hope they can also guide and support your journey.

CHAPTER 38

Trust in the universe

Throughout my life journey, I have come to learn that every painful and traumatising moment is also a gift. It's a chance for you to embrace, to learn and to grow.

After my many dark moments, I know this may seem so crazy or hard to believe, but it is true. It took me years to understand it, but I finally accepted it.

We experience real growth as a person every time we overcome a challenge or obstacle that life places in front of us.

Do not wish for your problems to disappear; wish to become bigger than your problems.

Until I realised this, I had no idea how to really stop and focus on anything other than my girls and how to have contact with them. I needed to trust in God and know that the universe has its ways to give back what you need, when you need it. You may not understand the timing.

You may call them miracles, the law of attraction or life lessons. I like to call them blessings that have yet to unfold.

When I did become aware that I needed to look inwards and focus on myself to heal and mend this tremendous wound, I needed to become the person that I always believed was inside of me.

I had to stop worrying so much about everybody else's expectations. I decided it was time to become the person that I deeply desired to blossom into. I watched the cherry blossom unfold its pink soft delicate petals and open to new beginnings again just as I was vulnerable to new experiences, yet here we were showing up.

There have been many times I have rested on my knees and asked for guidance. I have prayed for the reasons for me to be in this situation. I prayed that I would open my heart, soul and spirit to the divine and be guided. To be given a reason to continue living because there were many moments I couldn't see it.

The mere thought of putting my trust in the universe gave me the serenity and peace I so desperately searched for.

The power of continuous prayer, manifesting to a higher being, or whoever that may be for you is life-changing.

For me, God was one of my paths to the strength and belief in myself I hold today. I found peace in surrendering all my fears and have faith that my life would improve.

I also knew that was just the beginning, not only did I need to become humble,

I needed to have belief in myself that I could truly turn a new page and love myself enough to get up each and every day and be alive because I was enough. As much as my support group of family and friends loved me at the end of the day when it was just me in silence, in the discomfort of not knowing who I really was yet something began to change inside me. I didn't know what it was at first, acceptance I think is the best way to describe it. I took small steps like sparkles of light that shone from the sky. When things felt all too difficult to handle I'd stop what I was doing close my eyes and ask God for help.

CHAPTER 39

Asking for and accepting help

There were moments I felt so alone and distressed in my life. I didn't know who to turn to for help.

When I finally built up the courage to ask for help, I had to shut out the voice of my ego telling me I wasn't good enough, worthy enough, or loving enough to receive this help.

To move forward and heal, I had to leave aside the stories I made up in my head. I knew deep down there was no truth in these negative thoughts.

This was the time for me that I had to face reality.

This is when you have a choice.

If we deliberately stop and become aware of the pendulum swinging one way or the other, we always have a choice in what to believe or hear.

As hard as it may be to choose the path that seems more difficult to follow, it may turn out to be the better road travelled.

I began to notice that people were more than willing to lend me a hand to help. Once I took the initial step in asking the rest came in as if the wind had brought it. Sometimes it was manual labour, a friend's company, even a cheque for a generous amount and the advice of people whose wisdom of words were a tool for me to make better choices.

CHAPTER 40

Healing through meditation

I never imagined that very first meditation session would open up never-ending possibilities for me.

At first, the meditation I practised was inconsistent. Over time, I found I got better at sitting for prolonged periods and I began to feel relief and inner peace – even if it was just while I was meditating.

I gradually began to feel better about myself. I became aware of an inner void that was being met by focusing and being mindful of my surroundings.

Walking up the mountain and being in contact with my natural surroundings, I would discover something new every day. I was aware of the variety of native birds coming through, the shape of leaves and variety of colours, the temperature of the wind as it blew onto my face.

I was sitting still, both in mind and body, letting the tears run down my face. If you asked me why I was crying I couldn't tell you exactly. It was a series of sequences just like in a movie that I watched go by, it was the story of my life unfolding. It almost felt like there was a healing process taking place at that very moment.

I would repeat the mantra *Maranatha*, which at that moment I still had no idea what it meant. There were only a few things I had been able to retain in my memory, but I knew that having repeated it in the school lunch meditation, it could do me no harm. On the contrary, every time I repeated the word I felt healed in a small way.

Now I know (and love) the *Maranatha* mantra. *Maranatha* is an ancient word of Christian tradition and although the teachings of yoga meditation are non-sectoral, it was appropriately being used in a Christian school. Maranatha means 'Come Lord'.

Today I find myself more and more in tune, more mindful, of what is around me and am so grateful for that initial introduction from Diana to meditate. I set my alarm clock half an hour earlier every day to allow enough time to start the day off with my meditation. Some days it's Deepak Chopra, Jon Kabat-Zinn, Wayne Dyer, Marianne Williamson, Gabby Bernstein, Rebecca Campbell, downloaded on my phone, other days it may be Rob Ginnivan or my own meditation and sometimes I simply sit in silence. If I've missed my morning meditation I allow for some mindfulness colouring and yes some days it's ok to just sit in silence and take whatever natural surroundings you have even if for just a few minutes.

I place my mat in front of a large window in winter where I can see the trees and the beautiful colourful rosellas that visit and sing to me and I am so grateful.

In the warmer months I like to be barefoot and feel grounded to the earth while I feel the gentle breeze with my eyes shut.

I just think at the end of my meditation what a great start to the day and how blessed I am.

My weekly meditation group allows for a mixed bag of surprises. Each person takes turns and brings a different type of meditation. I see it as a gift to be shared.

If you are first starting to meditate don't feel discouraged or disturbed if you can't focus, any meditation will be helpful.

I LOVE WHO I AM Meditation

Breathe in deeply a couple of times. With each breath you take try to feel that a stream of energy is entering your body.

Think of yourself and see yourself in your mind

Allow this to sink into your eyes, your ears your crown, your neck, your chest, your arms all the way to your hands and fingertips.

Then go down to your stomach, feel your buttocks, your legs all the way down to your feet and toes.

Hold this space and be thankful for the body that has carried you this far and continues to do so.

Give yourself warm love to the parts of you that are holding resentment.

The parts that carry illness and hold anger. Like the seasons just as the trees, forever evolving, changing and releasing a shower of leaves onto the ground so do we let go of our fears, worries and sadness and embrace the *new experiences to come. The shoots that will in time be the beautiful flowers.*

Let it go…. Let it go…. Let it go

Find the most vulnerable part of yourself and see yourself caressing this area.

Feel compassion for yourself for all choices you've made good or bad and hold no judgement.

Stay in this space just a little longer with your eyes still closed physically hug yourself like you've never loved before and say out loud:

"I love who I am"

When you're ready, begin to come back to centre and open your eyes.

CHAPTER 41

Breaking free from fear and celebrating gratitude

Finding that place to breakthrough fear and hold the courage to be who you are, no matter who is present, is very difficult.

Even as I write this I know I am exposing myself completely – it takes an enormous amount of courage! Yet no matter what happens, I am at peace with myself, knowing there is a cause greater than myself. I hope sharing what I have learnt will help other women to take the same *first step to begin believing in themselves.*

There are days when fear is dreadfully present.

Some days I feel like I am being placed back on the rollercoaster ride for a split second, and it's during these days that I take a breath and I think about who might be needing my help today. I consciously shift my thoughts to that person. Sometimes I pause wherever I may be, even if I am in the supermarket aisle, and say a few calming words. I choose not to jump back on the rollercoaster of emotions.

Some mornings after meditating, I write a few words such as:

> *Today I am grateful for nature, the birds and the sun and for meeting Crystal. May she find the balance she seeks to be vulnerable with those she loves. Namaste.*

Namaste is a customary greeting used when arriving or departing.

I had to take some time to identify what scared me. To know what was blocking my path and stopping me from achieving what I wanted.

What to do when you are afraid

I've had to ask myself these questions:

What are you really scared of?

Is this a story you have heard before?

Has it helped you in any way in the past?

Why should you break free from this fear now?

The answers will come to you at some point when you are ready to hear them and trying to find answers on a really emotional day are best left to decide when you are feeling that you can use the rational part of your mind more.

Visualisations

See yourself at a river

There are leaves falling off the trees going down the stream. Place your concerns on a leaf and send it down the stream. Visualise you placing the problems on this leaf. It is so magically strong it can carry a mountain. Watch it go all the way down the It is the most peaceful of all places and so secure.

Seeing YOU in the future

See yourself in the future how you would like to be? Who are the people that surround you and uplift you? What are the things you need to do to get there and what is bringing you joy?

See yourself as a young child

You seek approval from yourself wanting and needing to be loved and nurtured. Remember seeing yourself in a photo when you were a baby or a 4 year old.

Tell this child how much you love her. Look into her eyes and tell her how special she is. Now ask her what she would like to do that would allow her to feel completely loved? Maybe she wants to go out with a friend, watch a movie, eat a pizza or simply just sleep in.

Listen with intention to what she needs and grant her this wish.

CHAPTER 42

My worthiness

Finding my own self-worth has been a lifelong search.

The first sign of acknowledgement was to be honest with myself and recognise where I was in my life. By this stage, I had given **everything** of myself to my family and my workplace.

I was exhausted, defeated.

The moment I recognised my marriage had ended, that it was time to move on, life did have new meaning. I did feel liberated.

But it took a long time to know my own worth.

There is an inspirational quote from Brenè Brown that resonates with me so much – yet it is so simple and has so much meaning:

I am enough.

To truly believe this, I couldn't just say it. I had to work on some aspects of my life to restore my love for myself.

So these are the actions I took:

- I tapped into my childhood and began to have fun again.
- I played and tried new adventures. I reluctantly rode in a rustic looking old go-cart left outside of the school. It was exhilarating and fun. It was like taking the inner child in me out for a fun adventure. I loved it!
- I planned trips with friends.
- I surrounded myself with positive people that accepted and supported me just the way I was.
- I was appreciative of the simple things in life and began to acknowledge them.

157

- I started walking around my streets and up the mountain every day.
- I listened to a friend's request for me to see a psychologist.
- I stopped worrying about what everyone else would think and followed my heart.
- I started eating well.
- I went dancing to salsa and cumbia (happy uplifting music).
- I dressed up just for me.
- I had bubble baths and played like a child making a mess
- I used aromatherapy oils with Neroli, Bergamot Lavender and frankincense.
- I stopped to have a really good look at my body, appreciated it and uncomfortably loved it at the beginning till I did it so many times I showered it with love.

CHAPTER 43

Forgiveness to be free

I walked into a church one day and there was nobody there except me.

My initial intention was to go in and ask for my girls' wellbeing and happiness. Then all of a sudden I had a great urge to cry and I could only think of Evan. They were mixed emotions. I felt a great sadness for him and all the awful feelings of anger I once had disappeared in that moment.

In their place there was empathy for what he was feeling and acknowledging the pain he was feeling too. I felt an immense sense of peace within myself and release from all the negative thoughts I had.

I realised I still cared for Evan. It was a different type of love I had once felt. I actually imagined him by my side holding his hand as a gesture of peace and affection.

By allowing myself the freedom to forgive Evan has given me the understanding to have empathy. As an example, whenever I am given the opportunity to drive Chloe somewhere or when I am dropping off Chloe at school, we talk about her Dad, and we share stories about when she was younger and the funny things her Dad did. She doesn't remember all the stories being so young but it makes her laugh and feel happy.

The other day she told me about Evan's visit to the dentist and how he insisted on the dentist giving him back his molar as a memento to take home to show the girls every intricate detail. We both laughed hysterically in the car.

The way I see it, there is no benefit to holding on to past pain and emotions.

We have to understand it is part of life's lesson and reflect on what it is we're meant to learn in the journey. I forgave myself as much as forgiving Evan.

Are you seeking to forgive? One lesson that I implemented was identifying 200 reasons for, or lessons learnt from, the painful event gradually writing them in a journal or voicing them in front of a mirror and how we have grown throughout the process. By finding at least 200 positive reasons for a negative event in your life changes your perspective and allows you to feel gratitude that you have been given this gift.

Most of us look at negative events and blame or get angry, but if you can turn your stressing into a blessing, it provides a completely different appreciation of the event that allows you to remain calm and at peace. Sometimes the negative emotion will come back into your head, but by writing all the positive outcomes, it will allow you to be able to replace the negative emotions with positive emotions quickly.

CHAPTER 44

Beauty and healing

In my early twenties I participated in a community beauty pageant. My ego was having a ball! I thought, 'Everyone is looking at me! This is real proof I must be beautiful if it has come down to only three of us amongst all these girls.'

I needed the acknowledgement of my outer beauty to feel loved and important to the world.

Often my relationships with people were so superficial. I used to judge others by their appearance, what they wore, analyse if they were symmetrically perfect when I would look at their faces.

I'd judge them if there was a hair out of place, if they were overweight or anything was seemingly imperfect.

I couldn't bear it if I found there were any imperfections in myself. This seemed to be all that mattered, even though I still wasn't happy.

True love and true beauty were only apparent to me when I began to look inward and appreciate who I was. I saw all the gifts I had inside of me that I had never been aware of.

It was the small and big gestures from people I didn't even know sometimes that made me reflect on my inner soul and then become aware of everyone else's beauty.

It wasn't until my 40th birthday that I really understood how beautiful I was without having to look at the reflection in the mirror. Now I look in the mirror and see a beautiful woman in every sense of the word, with all my virtues, grey hair, scars and fine lines around my face.

On my 41st birthday, my dear girlfriend Kim gave me Louise Hay's book, *You can heal your life*. This inspired me to do mirror work. In her book she says to stand in front of the mirror every day and say:

> *[Your name], I love you, I really, really love you.*

This can feel like too much to begin with, so an alternative to start with is:

> *[Your name], I am willing to learn to love you.*

I had bought myself a large framed mirror which was still boxed up in the garage waiting for the right moment when we bought our home to use. I thought about the number of things we buy and keep for the future and how some of those things never get used and end up in a charity store.

This was one of those a-ha moments, so I immediately took action and went into the garage and found the large mirror, unwrapped it and placed it in my bedroom.

I softly repeated the words 'I love you'. I sat in front of that mirror for a very long time – I lost track of time.

This has become a daily ritual. It's how I start my day. It is part of my meditation. Sometimes I add a sticky coloured post-it note to remind me to be kind to myself.

This is not a mood board or where I keep my family photos or goals. They have their place on the other side of the bedroom wall.

My mirror is an area for self-love.

I now love who I am – in every way possible.

Healing has become part of my day, helping the women at the nearby refuge by teaching them what I've learnt makes my day. Seeing their sad faces with tears running down their cheeks coming to terms with the pain they have held onto. Going through the process of transformation and finally seeing hope and knowing that the answers are in themselves. That there is always a choice.

The other part of my healing is through Reiki Self –treatment. This is a holistic approach to health through a gentle, loving touch I am able to nourish my body wherever I am. Particularly when I am stressed and may be in pain. Being intuitive since I was 8 years old and always wanting to help people made the decision to become a Reiki practitioner as if it was what I was always meant to be doing. I enjoy seeing people come in for a session and release all the baggage they carry, relief from their ailments, reduce their anxiety and help cope with their day.

CHAPTER 45

Unleash the power within

Steve and I married in 2014.

A few months later, my wonderful husband bought tickets for me to spend a weekend with Tony Robbins at his event *Unleash the Power Within*. I had never been to one of his events and felt guilty he had spent a lot of money, so I went along without any real intention of wanting to be there.

I can honestly say it changed my life.

The first day we queued for about 30 minutes. When it was our turn to register, the nice man on the other side of the table smiled at me and asked if I had been to the event before. He wished us well and not much more was said.

While this was happening I wondered why someone would want to give up their Friday morning as a volunteer to stand around and put wrist bands on everyone.

The first few hours I was bombarded with positive greetings from many different people in the room that I had never even met. I found it hard to understand why someone would want to be so friendly and nice without getting anything in return. I felt as if there was a catch and at any given moment something would be asked from me in return. Well, it never happened.

Who was this Tony Robbins guy? The moment he came out on stage there was this tremendous energy in his voice but it wasn't just that, it was also the wise words he had to say, his genuine thoughts and his big heart.

There was this contagious feeling of wanting to feel happy because everyone else was and without noticing it, I went from a state of uncertainty and sadness to feeling really happy about life. Surely all the jumping around, mini-massages I received and gave, and the reprogramming of my limiting beliefs must have had something to do with it?

I don't think I have ever felt so pumped and alive! Being in a space with more than 3000 people for four days with little food and sleep, yet feeling so enthusiastic and in love with life was incredible.

This was the beginning of a whole new way of thinking for me. The seed had been planted a while ago, but it took this moment for the petal to drop and for me to realise that my life had new meaning. I am now so grateful to be alive.

When you have a massive life awakening like I did, there is a certain discomfort you feel. For me it was like I was uncomfortable in my own skin because I was thinking outside the box for the first time in my life. I had never been challenged before about what

I believed. I just thought that what I believed was true because it was what I knew. For the first time someone was now asking, 'Why do you believe that? Where did that come from?'

I was now asking myself about my own beliefs. Not my parents' beliefs they had passed onto me, but what did I believe?

I began asking myself, 'What is my passion?'

This took me years to find my passion, and this *Unleash the power within* event gave me the drive to push myself further and truly believe that I could make massive changes in my life.

> *There is always room in your life for thinking bigger, pushing limits and imagining the impossible. – Tony Robbins*

CHAPTER 46

Beliefs about vulnerability

I always equated the word vulnerable with weakness. I saw it as your worst moment, and this in turn allowed others to attack you or take advantage of the circumstances. I saw it as a negative.

After reading *Daring Greatly* by Brenè Brown, it changed my whole perspective of the word and its meaning.

I now see vulnerability as an important, life-changing awareness. I hope my examples of being vulnerable can change your perception of the value of being vulnerable.

To me, vulnerability is:

- Waking up after a divorce and reaching out to your ex with open arms.
- Allowing a helping hand from a man and trusting him after being abused by men.
- Allowing your child to make mistakes when you know they are headed that way, without reaching in to save them so they can learn from their own mistakes.
- Forgiving someone you have disconnected with for a long time.
- Going on a first date after a divorce.
- Sharing your most vulnerable experience with someone worthy of listening to you.
- Giving life a second chance after attempting suicide.
- Following your heart and trusting God or the Universe even when the path seems lonely and your mind is saying to follow the crowd.
- Accepting the trials you receive and being present even when you are raw and grieving.

- Standing up for yourself.
- Falling in love.
- Trying something new.
- Admitting to being afraid.

Now standing at the other side of what felt like a tunnel, a symbol for my life's journey, and seeing the light at the end, I can see I had a choice. I could allow myself to be drowned in sorrow, despair and continue to feel sorry for myself and choose the quickest fix to rid myself of the pain. I could continue an endless vicious circle of pain or opt for the road less driven, the one I feared but had faith in with eyes closed, because deep in my heart, I knew it was the best way forward.

I stopped telling myself I wasn't worth it and I stood courageously. Did I fall over? Yes, again and again. I still do but it won't ever stop me from continuing the same path towards enlightenment.

What was different this time? I was totally aware I had hit rock bottom. I accepted things for what they were: I was a mother without her daughters.

I was for the first time embracing who I really was and what I was no longer prepared to put up with. No more abusive words from the man who had claimed to love me.

From that moment of acceptance and vulnerability, I started looking after my wounded soul. I was learning to know what I liked and could finally discuss what felt shameful – the mistakes I had made and what had kept me in the dark.

Being vulnerable with a selected few people allowed me to be at peace and let the shame pour out into the earth to be recycled.

CHAPTER 47

Six needs of the ego

One of the biggest lessons I learnt was how our ego plays a part in our lives. Our ego is designed for one reason — To protect us at all cost. The ego works from a place of fear. It lives in the mind and is where we turn to when protecting ourselves from others.

Have you been in an argument where you could not stop yourself, or you got really angry with someone, only to realise a few hours later, that it was all blown out of proportion. That is your ego driving you.

To know if you are coming from a place of authenticity, ask yourself if you are

STORM HIDEAWAY

speaking from the heart with love and kindness or are you speaking out to prove yourself.

If you speak from the heart you will be understood. It's a place of acceptance. We can take full responsibility for our actions.

This is called above-the-line thinking. It is a place where you are 100% responsible for your life. You can choose how you feel, how you respond and how you behave. You have all the choices on how you feel.

- You can choose to be angry or you can choose forgiveness.
- You can choose to be right or can choose to be understanding.
- You can choose to get even or can choose to let it go.
- You can choose to follow your heart or follow the expectations of the herd.

My ego fed on fear for years. I came from a place of below-the-line thinking. I took on the role of the martyr, I would lay blame on others and not take responsibility for my part.

The ego also has a need for drama. It wants things to be messed up so that it can play a role and keep you busy. Most people meet this need for drama in an ineffective way and get involved in bigotry, hatred, gossip, arguing, casting their opinions when not asked for, making judgements and simply pulling others down to make themselves feel better.

On a more positive note, we can have these needs met through a healthy outlet. I seek my need for drama from a TV show called *The Bachelor*. It allows me to escape from my everyday life. If you suppress it, it can come out in explosive ways.

There are 6 needs that your ego feeds off and I will highlight each of these:

The need to Justify

This need is met when you feel that you need to explain yourself to your partner. Driven out of fear of being judged, you will feel it is important to explain why or why not you did, or did not do something.

Often we made a mistake, or forgot to do something. We need to apologise for the error, but do not feel you need to justify it. That is the ego talking.

The Need to Know

This need is often on the other end of the need to Justify. When someone does something unexpected and it impacts on you, or not to your liking, you become a detective, wanting to know all the answers. If the person has apologised, then let it go and trust them. Wanting to know all the reasons, not only makes the other person feel bad, but it also demonstrates a lack of trust.

Sometimes we have a need to know something for safety reasons, but remember to ask yourself if you are coming from the heart or from the head.

The Need to Look Good

Our need to look good is driven by our requirement to be accepted and belong. We want to look good in front of our friends and family and often people will use sarcasm and laughter at the expense of others or worse, their partner.

We can use this need of looking good as an example to others. Be the caring, compassionate and understanding person. The person who looks out for others to help them and not belittle them.

The Need to Get Even

The Ego's need to get even is probably one of the most destructive needs. This need come from a place of entitlement or belief that everything should be fair and that we have the right to do unto others. The problem with this need is that it never ends. You will often see this in arguments. He says one thing, so you want to say something more hurtful to get even. Then he will reply more hurtful again.

You know when this need has been used, because you will find yourself apologising for what you said and that you did not mean it. The ONLY time you want the need to get even, is when your partner has done something caring and loving for you and you want to get even in being loving back.

The Need to be Right

The need to be right will stop you from ending an argument and saying sorry. If your ego is yelling at you that you are right, how in the world do you say sorry? Often you may find yourself in a position where you forget about what you were arguing over and find yourself discussing who was right and who was wrong. The challenge is to take ourselves out of that situation and be at peace with it. At the end of the day it does not matter when love is involved.

The Need to Judge

Our need to judge others comes from a place of insecurity and trying to make ourselves feel better.

None of us are perfect and I believe that every one of us is trying to do the best we can with the resources and information available to us. If we could do better; we would. If we knew better, we would do things differently.

To overcome this need, forget worrying so much about other

people's faults and look for the good in people.

All our needs of the ego are a part of us and they can be fulfilled by healthy means – with above-the-line thinking.

When thinking below-the-line, the ego holds us back from truly being open to growing into who we can become.

Things in life are forever changing. It is our limitations to change that stop us and becomes painful because we resist rather than just letting go.

> *When you allow your ego to control your thoughts everything you believe in becomes an illusion.* – *Rusty Eric*

Steps for removing Ego from your day.

1. Recognise that when things become stressful, that the ego will start to become active.

2. When placed in a stressful situation, try and remove yourself from it.

3. If possible, try and become objective in assessing the situation and less emotional.

4. Identify the need (or 2) that is being met in this moment and ask yourself 'Am I coming from a place of love and compassion, or am I focussing on me?'

   Author, Joe Pane

CHAPTER 48

Affirmations for my empty nest

After our unsuccessful IVF attempt, I did accept my empty nest.

Today I am grateful for the stronger woman it made me. I am grateful for the strong relationship I hold with Steve and most of all, I feel for all the women out there who have gone through this time and time again.

To accept and adjust to my life without my children, I use these affirmations:

- I love who I am

- I am grateful for the abundance I receive each day.
- I am grateful for new life inside me.
- I am willing to release any unworthy thoughts from my body.
- I am willing to nurture this new life in the comfort of my womb.
- I hold loving protection for my child and me.
- All is well in my womb.
- I am protected by God, the angels, the universe.
- I am enough, I am worthy of whatever the universe, angels, and God sends me.
- I am the light needed to guide this new spirit in me.
- I am fulfilled and ready to receive this gift with every molecule in my body.
- I am love multiplied.
- I am grateful for being alive and await patiently whatever is to come.
- I release any agony, pain, frustration, anger, and depression I hold.

- I have self-compassion for what I am going through.
- I hold myself warmly and say I love you Storm.
- I am complete
- I am receiving abundantly
- I am worthy of love from my community
- I am a healer
- I am worthy of loving myself
- I am enough without carrying a child in my womb

———— ❀ ————

CHAPTER 49

My wall of courage

On my bedroom wall I have a collection of photos of people I love and that mean the world to me.

On it are my beautiful girls – mostly when they were younger because these are the times they allowed me to photograph them.

I also have photos of other loved ones as well as affirmations and words of encouragement.

My daily mantra is:

> *I Storm Hideaway, hear, feel, see and know that the purpose of my life is to be a loving, giving and passionate*

person so I can be an example to my daughters and others.

I believe every quality you admire about the people you see around you is inside you. You just have to allow yourself to be aware, to let the light shine on you so you are able to see these qualities in you.

I know this may seem impossible to some, but if you are willing to let go of the belief that you are not capable and instead invite the chance these beliefs may be true and things may be different, then things start to change.

When you can begin to live the way you want – even when you find it hard to believe in yourself – you are a step closer. It takes work and daily practice.

I wish there was a quick fix, but this isn't the case. It takes courage to see where you are at and be willing to let go and give up the things that are holding you back.

I had to ask myself what is stopping me from achieving my goals and being a courageous person – what is stopping me being the best version of myself?

It takes courage to acknowledge that God loves you just the way you are and made you beautiful with all your imperfections.

Letting go of what people think about me has been one of my greatest challenges, yet I feel I am in a better place. I care less about my thoughts on what others may be thinking or saying about me.

After all we cannot stop people from doing this but I can stop worrying about how I react. In exchange it has given me peace and allowed me to be more authentic.

CHAPTER 50

My other mother

I like to explain this as an invisible bubble, a divine light that shines light on me. No one else can see it but it is definitely there. The more mindful I am of the bubble, the better it protects me from situations where I may be vulnerable.

You may want to call it a second mother, always watching out for you. You see, sometimes we allow so much information in and take on other people's problems without even noticing it. Trying so hard to fix things and absorbing negative energy without really noticing the consequences later.

By no means am I saying we shouldn't help people, but if we allow everyone in without a pause, a moment to look after ourselves, then we have forgotten to take care of ourselves first.

How do I notice this is happening to me? The small things that generally don't irritate me begin to. I snap for no apparent reason. I yell at the people I love the most when it isn't their fault.

In more extreme situations I only have to look back at my past and notice that my defence mechanism was to be numb to all the inflicted pain and pretend nothing was wrong. This only led to attracting more negative people to tell me their problems and believe it was OK because I was allowing it.

I would hesitate to answer the phone if I knew it was going to be someone wanting to gossip or having to listen to their problems for an hour. I didn't know how to stop these situations from occurring.

The difference now is I know myself well enough to choose what or who I listen to and be prepared to simply walk away. Carefully selecting the people I choose to spend my time with has paid off, and those people that can be a burden, I have chosen to see less of.

CHAPTER 51

Love is what matters

It all comes back to love.

Even when you are missing love in your life, or your relationship isn't working well, the first person you need to work on is **yourself**.

I had to be willing to release any harsh judgements.

I used to tell myself I was ugly and awful and not worthy to be around. I also used to say I was a piece of shit. None of this language was helping me and no wonder I was in the place I was in.

Mirror work was a good place to start for me.

193

Then focusing on doing something I enjoy, such as getting a massage or having my nails done, or watching a movie on my own.

It's important to take time out to value yourself.

We so easily let this slip and put ourselves last when it should be a priority.

> *You can't give away what you don't have. – Wayne Dyer*

It's also valuable to release any negative thoughts you may have towards your ex-partner and send them good thoughts.

When you first practice this it may be really hard to do. It can feel uncomfortable, yet the more you practice, the easier it becomes. Even if you don't believe it, if it comes from a place of good intention, things can shift.

Here are some affirmations I have created and use:

- I am willing to release the anger and resentment I have towards my partner.

- I am willing to receive love and give love unconditionally.
- I am willing to give of myself without resentment.
- I am willing to forgive [name].
- I am willing to try something new even when it feels uncomfortable.
- I am willing to love myself.
- I am willing to receive love abundantly.
- I love who I am.
- I love my imperfections.
- I love my body exactly the way it is
- I embrace all my personal gifts.
- I am willing to forgive myself for _____
- I am lovable.
- I receive love throughout the day.
- I am worthy of love.
- I am in love with myself.
- I love the person I am now.
- I love myself without ifs or buts.
- I am deeply loved by all of life.

Always Here (A letter to my daughters)

As I write these words I feel discomfort in my throat. I'm using a pencil, you once wrote with Chloe, when you were 9 years old. I've kept it all these years.

I want you to both know that I've always been here for both of you. I don't know why I feel this guilt. My mind must be playing games on me. The truth is I have always been here for you.

I have been blamed for not giving you enough, for not being perfect enough. The truth is, I am enough and so are you. You are a beautiful creation of God.

You are a reflection of what I have always dreamed my daughters would be since you were in my womb. I was there when you were born, when you took your first step, when your first tooth came out, when you smiled, when you went to school for the first time.

I was here in spirit every mother's day, every birthday and every Christmas. I was also here when you cried, when you got excited, when you went on your first date, when you got your license and when you finished school.

I was here when you felt alone and thought you had no friends and couldn't count on anyone.

I was right here all along with you in your heart every moment excited to hug you, kiss you and tell you that I love you.

Mum xxxxx

EPILOGUE

There are still wounds that have not healed and may never heal.

However I am now sure of the things I have control over. My life is better because I am in control of it now. I decide when I wake up and how to take on the day.

I do have sad days, but now most of them are fantastic because I make a choice each moment of every day to have joy in my life. I choose happiness, love and friendships.

Life is abundant. I live in an amazing place. Before my feet touch the ground of a morning, I wake up and am happy because I have a warm bed to sleep on.

I have an outstanding relationship and there is love in my life.

My family accept me for who I am and stand beside me through everything. I am grateful to share special moments including my parents, my brothers and my nieces and nephew.

I am grateful for gradual miracles that occur daily with my daughters when I drive them to school each morning.

I am mindful of the warm sun on my face, the fresh air that I breathe and the moments I meditate.

I am thankful for friendships and the good Samaritans who have given me a hand without knowing who I really was.

I am grateful for the women I can help through the pain I have overcome.

There are now certain times that are not negotiable: the time I give myself. I have learnt that without this time, I don't function well and therefore I can be of little help to those I love. This time is spent on meditation, exercise, or stimulating my brain with useful positive information. Sometimes this comes in the form of reading a book, a post or affirmations.

Once these have been fulfilled, there is time for work and giving of myself to others.

I notice the days I miss this important time, I don't function as well as I could. I place it back in my daily routine as soon as possible.

If you have noticed the errors in the book you are forgiving enough to know they were deliberately left there for you to notice perfection doesn't exist.

My wish is that no matter your struggles or challenges, you will make time every day to give back to yourself.

Please make time to love YOU.

When you love yourself, you can be the very best version of yourself.

Printed in the United States
By Bookmasters